Diary of a
Juvenile Delinquent

Diary of a Juvenile Delinquent

STEVEN BERKOFF

A MEMOIR

BOOKS

In memory of my beloved mother Polly.

First published in Great Britain in 2010 by
JR Books, 10 Greenland Street, London NW1 0ND
www.jrbooks.com

A catalogue record for this book is available from the British Library.

ISBN 978-1-907532-08-5

1 3 5 7 9 10 8 6 4 2

Printed and bound by Clays Ltd, St Ives plc

66I think we all have an obsession to peep into the distant past and not just our own, but others whose lives have sunk into oblivion. When I look at the photographs enshrined now in museums and catalogues, of my pre-world, I find I am filled with a terrible nostalgia for a world I never knew, and yet feel haunted by. I frequently dip into my own childhood memories and para-doxically as I age the early memories seem to grow clearer, as if, now, I perhaps understood myself a little more.

Childhood is a somewhat reckless time when you are tipped into the great ocean's wave and guide yourself as best you can to some friendly shore. In my particular case, some shores were quite hostile, however with that incredible optimism that seems to be the birthright of all but the most brutalised children, we just keep going, trusting somehow that our instincts will lead us to sweet and nourishing havens.**99**

Steven Berkoff

Contents

Part I

As a Child

Who knows how I got here? It's a complete mystery to me how I ended up in a small flat in 104 Whitechapel Road, London E1 in 1937. It was a hot summer, so they tell me. Ma and Pa were born here in the East End and I know that when she was a child, Ma lived in Batty Street, buildings that surprisingly still exist. The East End was packed full of Jews then, with estimates of about 150,000 – which is an awful lot crushed into one area, and what a bizarre and fascinating area it was. From what I gather from my investigations, sporadic reading and bits of info from Uncle Sam (Dad's younger brother, who lived in Cannon Street Road, off Commercial Road), Ma's family came from Odessa (on the Black Sea) and had been living quite a prosperous, even creative life until Tsar Nicholas I came to power (1825–55) and started to crush down on the Jews, creating 600 new laws affecting them which is a hell of a lot to have to deal with and while oppressing them, paradoxically made them a whole lot shrewder and far more cunning, as they would need to be, even to survive! The most horrible law of all was the conscription of children from the age of eight to be trained until old enough to serve in the

Armed Forces, an unbelievable 25 years. That was a terrible period when children were often just snatched from their homes and rarely saw their parents again. Alexander II abolished this law, thank God, when he came to power.

But that was only a brief period of liberalism and after Alexander's assassination in 1881, things got pretty bad for my family and there was a terrible pogrom (a Russian word meaning devastation), which took place in 1871. This seems to have been the turning point for many Jews to look west – which they did in huge numbers, especially during the reign of Tsar Nicholas II (1894–1917). He ushered in an era of state-supported pogroms and devastation on a scale beyond imagination until of course the Nazis improved on it. The first was the inferno in 1881–82, followed by more in 1903 and 1905. I believe it was during the one in 1882 when my family upped stakes and fled – and how they fled since more than two million Jews left Russia between 1880 and 1920.

The persecutors forced them to flee for whatever reason (of course there were always many of these) by instigating a pogrom. The pogroms fired up the local population to make them believe the Jews were responsible for killing Tsar Alexander or taking over major industries, or being revolutionaries or ruthless capitalists – you name it, the Jews did it. The Cossacks, slaughterers acting for the Tsar, would sweep into a Jewish village and set fire to major buildings and synagogues. One of their favourite tricks, all good sabre practice, was to lop off the ears of any Jew unlucky enough to get in their way. Of course my mother's family – the Hymans – had to leave and so they did, which was fortunate since things got a lot worse before they got better, only to get worse again when 36,000 Jews were machine-gunned in Odessa in 1941.

It must have been a madhouse trying to get out but escape they did and at the Odessa port boarded old ships financed by charitable organisations in London and New York. As they swept westwards, they never gazed back on the accursed home country of lunatic Tsars, crazy laws and thick, brutal Russian peasants. Instead they looked to the West and dreamt of a better world. Just a few years later (in 1905), 690 pogroms were carried out, which encouraged a few more (100,000) Jews to head west. Of course none of them could speak a word of English and so they relied on the goodwill of those who greeted them at the London docks, which many were told was New York. They disembarked innocently, believing they had arrived at the promised land of America (this might be a little far-fetched since they only had to ask a more enlightened traveller but you never know what a massive crowd of frightened, hysterical Russian Jews would be capable of believing). The Russian refugees turned up in every capital of the world however, including Paris, London, Berlin, Vienna and Stockholm. Apart from Vienna and Berlin, which weren't too friendly to Jewish refugees, they were given sympathetic receptions.

There were institutions for the refugees to rest their heads before they found work and shelter but my maternal grandfather soon became employed in the fish business (pickling and salting) and eventually opened up a small grocery store. On my father's side they swiftly fell into the ritual trade for those whose tongues are silent and that is tailoring. London's East End became the tailoring capital of England and my dad, like all his brothers, was educated in sweatshops so dusty and unventilated that sadly, two of them lost their sight in their late-sixties.

The East End was naturally the first port of call and soon it became a mini replica of a Polish-Jewish shtettle (ghetto) with the added difference that one could leave just by getting on a bus. Jewish delis and markets sprouted everywhere to satisfy every taste, as well as theatres where the actors played in Yiddish. Soon they became famous and Jewish actors from all over the world would come and play there.

And so here I was born in 1937, just 50 years after that night in Odessa when my grandparents packed their bags and left everything else behind. They brought nothing but their culture, their ideas and their incredible hopes – and England did not let them down.

My mother was the last of 11 children, who were born in Stepney, east London between 1880 and 1902. Father was the eldest of six, who were born between virtually the same period and so at one time I had 19 uncles and aunts and I can recall only a few of them. Between my large and scattered family, little vignettes would suddenly surface: since all my uncles and aunts had children I had around 50 cousins, who I never stopped meeting or hearing about – for example, my mother talked fondly about her sister Kitty, who had a beautiful singing voice but died early. I learned of a Sam on my mother's side, who was one of the earliest migrants to New York. He swiftly gained knowledge of the ways of the underworld and became a bootlegger. Inordinately wealthy, he sent for the rest of the family to join him in New York. He was small, stocky and powerful and for some reason that I was never told, he called himself Sam Senate. An extremely tough guy, according to Ma he once wrestled with the great German strongman, George Hackenschmidt.

Another of Ma's many brothers, also part of the hard brigade, was my dear Uncle Alf. He too changed his name, to Mansfield and became one of the toughest, fastest flyweights on the planet, narrowly losing to legendary Welshman Jimmy Wilde in a World Title bout in the early twenties – at Holborn Stadium. However, after one too many bashings he was fast losing his eyesight, first in one eye and then the other. Unbelievably, he continued to fight and eventually went completely blind. I remember him as always being full of humour and gifted with wonderful stories – he even mocked his own blindness. The man was nothing less than heroic and never once complained about his plight, but as a child I sometimes found his mauled face somewhat difficult to gaze on. His nose was completely mashed, his lips swollen and misshapen; his eyes pale and flecked. He always wore a very smart suit, though and his shoes were well polished. To earn his own living and not be a burden on others, he would sell black market chocolate in the West End 'Speilers' (gambling dens) during the war.

I also liked Uncle Jack, who lived with his lovely wife off the Hackney Road. Many a time Ma and I would visit one-eyed Jack (blindness seemed to run in the family). He was apparently the youngest male and had had a hard young life – when all the family emigrated to New York in the early twenties, for some reason he was put into a home. Now he was just a sweet, gentle guy. Ma's second-oldest brother, Uncle Joe, emigrated for Australia and joined the army, where he thrived in the infantry. Pretty soon he had enough, though and joined his family in New York. Blind boxer Alf was married and had a lovely daughter called Paula, who was destined for show business and worked at it all her life – unsuccessfully, unfortunately. Although she had a lot of guts, she just didn't seem to find her niche. In middle age she did, however, score a big hit in a commercial for toilet paper, strange as that may sound. Having found it so outrageous, she then turned the experience into a one-woman show. On my first visit back to New York in 1974, I saw it one afternoon with an invited (and slightly embarrassed) audience.

But Paula did get lucky in the end and she found the most wonderful guy called Chet, who was an architect. He was so accommodating that he actually relished doing all the chores for Paula and their two kids. They had a lovely girl called Laura, with whom I became quite friendly (and still am). On my father's side there were also some strange and exotic people but I will mention them later. Except for my other Uncle Sam (Dad's brother), whom I grew to love and respect as much, if not more than my own father. Sam was an adventurer who, in the twenties sailed to New York and lived there for a few years, doing odd jobs at first. He was a disciple of John Dos Passos, Upton Sinclair and Ernest Hemingway. Sam had a tremendous intellect and could quote reams of Shakespeare; he worked his whole life as a trouser cutter until he too unbelievably went blind. He never drank, never smoked, loved endless cups of tea and sandwiches and had a story to tell every day of the year.

Dad's part of the family came from Bucharest, Romania. They were all of quite a dark complexion with jet black curly hair, saturnine, fond of the good life, food – and most of all – gambling. Gambling seemed to be in their blood, but it never attracted my Uncle Sam, who was more interested in books, politics, ideas and communism. Indeed, Sam was an ardent communist, as were most East-End Jews, until Russia's brutal crushing of the Hungarian uprising in 1956 – then he had had enough. Sam was a worker, with strong beliefs in the decency and ethical treatment of the working classes; he had a strange way of speaking – half-preaching, half-joking. He and my father could not be more different. Dad had his nose in the racing results while Sam's nose was in *Das Kapital*. Sam is featured in an extraordinary mural in Cable Street that celebrates the workers preventing Oswald Mosely and his army of fascists from getting through the streets of the East End in 1936.

In the beginning I vaguely remember a pram and being carried up a flight of stairs – the pram was left on the landing. I recall this since it must have been the most-repeated action on a daily basis to our flat on the first floor in Whitechapel Road, Stepney. There is also a shadowy memory of an Underground station and being whipped away in the night when the demon sirens went off. As fate would have it, our house in Whitechapel was the only one that night in 1942 to receive a direct hit. We'd gone to the Underground shelter in Whitechapel. Dad didn't want to go, Mum told me (the siren had gone off for 20 consecutive nights and each one had been a false alarm). He said: 'The kids are sleeping so peacefully, so let them be.' But Ma insisted, even if that meant dragging us all out again on another false call.

I owe my life to Ma in more ways than one: my sister Beryl once told me how I was conceived. Ma desperately wanted another child but Dad didn't, hence the long gap between us of seven years (Beryl was born in 1930). So Ma stuck a pin through the tip of his contraceptives. Dad never knew about this little trick but I think somehow he felt betrayed and didn't welcome me with any enthusiasm. However, I was what Ma wanted above all: a boy, a blue-eyed boy, who looked just like her – I was her treasure and she never let me forget it.

And now for a memory I have never been able to push from my mind. When Ma left me at the children's home (she deposited me temporarily after the bombing before we were re-housed), the matron gave me a green apple. I suppose it was to comfort me but I was so distressed to see Ma leave that I howled non-stop for days. No longer able to cope with such a whining brat, the matron sent for Ma to pick me up. That sour green apple seemed to symbolise the whole experience.

The next memory was of a three-wheeled, tiny red bike that I'd ride round and round the living room in the small town of Luton in Bedfordshire where we were evacuated. I must have been about four years old at the time. Since I was always up early, it was dark in Luton and by then a fire was roaring and the radio was on, always with the same news: that the RAF had shot so many German planes out of the sky. Of course we were always winning because we were the good guys and I was too young to feel anything for the poor German boys blown apart, fighting a worthless war for a tyrant.

In those days I shared a single bedroom with my sister so we slept head to toe and it was around this time that I experienced the first twinges of sex. Soon after I got my own room. My bed was against the wall and I could stare out at a tree, which seemed to be growing from a compost heap. There was little else in the room. The bathroom was next door to it and my big bath night was on Friday, when I would feel exceptionally clean for several days. I do recall my first day in this rented house in Grantham Road because for some reason I stuck my head between the wooden poles of the small gate and my parents had to ask a neighbour to saw me out. I remember that incident well! During the mass evacuation from London in the early days of the War, Beryl, my sister had been housed with a nice lady in Crewe with whom she formed a life-long attachment. This lady posted her books to educate her to a wider world and I always remember one of them being by Mark Twain.

By chance, my Aunty Ray (Ma's sister who lived in Nyack, New Jersey) had a son called Morris, who was in the American forces and stationed over here. He'd visit quite frequently and was a source of immense pleasure to me since he always came laden with food parcels bought from the army stores and also brought loads of toys for me, which were wondrous in their mechanical possibilities. It was he who taught me how to tell the time since my dad taught me nothing – and anyway, I didn't possess a watch then. Morris was a gentle soul who did pharmaceutical work for the army and I was always overjoyed when he visited since he never ceased to talk to me and make a fuss of me.

Ray was one of eight brothers and sisters who emigrated to New York from the East End with Ma and Pa, who in fact got married out there in the twenties. As I have already mentioned, my rich Uncle Sam sent for them all after he made a fortune in the bootlegging business and changed his name to Senate. In the early 1920s he paid for the rest of the family to come out and join him. That's where I might have been born, had Dad not wanted to go back to London to help look after his ailing Ma and Pa, the Berkowitz's (my mother's side were the more adventurous Hymans). But the Hymans never returned to England and yet Ma never ceased longing to go back to New York, where she and her husband had lived for four years. She was eager to be reunited with her family and in those days the talk was of how we were going back to America after the war – everything was 'after the war'.

Our landlady in Luton was of another era altogether and still wore long black Victorian gowns. Her name was Miss Everet and she came once a week to collect the rent and check the house. She had locked up the front room for herself and her private belongings and each time she unlocked the door I would dash in since there was an upright piano in there. Nothing gave me more pleasure than to pound away on it, which she didn't seem to mind at all. Although my passion never ceased and even grew more intense, it never occurred to Ma to get me piano lessons since the excuse was always 'after the war' and when the war was over, it was 'after we get to America'. I was becoming used to rejection as if it was a natural way of life. Of course I hated it, but I also accepted it as one of the penalties for not being an adult – I hate it just as much today.

The first sign that I had grown up enough to be endowed with a smidgen of responsibility was one day when Ma asked me to go round the corner to the grocery store to buy some flour. Thrilled to be entrusted with such a responsibility I clutched the sixpenny piece and dashed there and back with great pride.

The first day of school came and for the second time in my life I saw Ma walking away from me, though this time I was a five-year-old and able to handle it a bit better. As soon as our mothers left the room, the teacher swiftly provided distraction by teaching us the alphabet, getting us to painstakingly chalk the letters on our small blackboards, but I was still glad when lunchtime came and Ma collected me. Together we walked home, which was thankfully just round the corner from Maidenhall School. The days passed pleasantly enough at that small institution but sometimes to amuse themselves the kids would knot the end of their scarves, surround me and shout out 'Jewboy!' It really didn't bother me too much for that was how their imaginations responded to what they had been taught in religious instruction and their actions may have also been slightly inflamed by the two other Jews in the school, who took the 'holy' days off. This somewhat embarrassed me since those days meant nothing to me at the time because Dad paid no attention to them – though Jewish, his upbringing was far too secular for the niceties of religious rituals, but it also made it a little difficult to develop any real friendships during those years at primary school.

I recall one of the Jewish boys' names: he was called Neville Blech. He wore thick lens glasses and scored top marks in just about every subject; there seemed to be nothing that he couldn't do. I used to stare at him with a certain amount of envy. During the morning and afternoon break we would play marbles and I coveted my collection of those beautiful and mysterious spheres.

Once a month Ma took me to the barber across the road from the school to have my hair trimmed for 10 pence. She always gave him a shilling and I never knew why I didn't get the two pence back! Next door was a sweet shop, which sold yellow twigs that had been soaked in some kind of liquorice, and I'd chew them until there was no flavour left – I think they were meant to be good for children's teeth. Anyway, we were rationed for everything and this was a good substitute. A few doors down was the small fish and chip shop, which sold the most divine chips. Ma would give me a threepenny bit to buy a small bag, but they were always stuffing the chips in a bag so small that they tumbled out onto the newspaper. I suppose it made them look 'generous'.

In the summer when I grew older my sister took me swimming at our local lido, something I looked forward to so much. I recall that she took me with her to the women's changing room since I was still so small, but one day she was told that I had to go to the men's changing room – quite a daunting experience since I didn't have a clue what I should do. Some kindly older boys guided me and this was another small rite of passage when I had to learn to stand on my own feet. I loved going to the lido more than just about anything and though I couldn't yet swim, I paddled round with a pair of yellow water wings. One day I just let them go and found that I could still float, which completely amazed me – I never stopped swimming after that.

The next stage of course was the diving board: I soon got used to jumping and springing off and doing somersaults. I remember feeling little fear as if I knew that nothing really bad could happen to me – you just have to be a little daring sometimes. Soon I ventured up to the higher boards and eventually to the very top one, which had a sign up: 'Expert Divers Only'. The pool looked so very far away, but still I jumped and lo and behold, I was in one piece! It wasn't long after that when I dived. Sometimes Ma would come and then she would proudly watch me.

I loved the salad sandwiches that you could buy in the little restaurant there. At that time a few prisoners of war were also pounding up and down the pool and these young German men looked so fit and handsome and in fact, many of them were blond. Unless they were higher-ranking soldiers with special privileges, it wasn't so bad then. Even when it was baking hot, Dad seldom came. Beryl and I would stay all day and then walk back through the maze of streets until we reached home, which was now in Highfield Road.

We had moved to a slightly larger house although it was still quite a small, Edwardian-style building in a street where every home was identical. I now made friends for the first time with two children who lived opposite me, called John and Janet Ellis. They were decent, well brought up kids of the lower middle class and it was through Janet that I felt the first pangs of what I thought were the stirrings of love. I was longing to tell her, but in the end I never could. With her thick plait falling down her back, she was so pretty. John, Janet and me would play in the grounds of Frickers, a large factory nearby. We dragged some rusty old oil drums into a square, laid corrugated metal over them and that was our den. There we fantasised and chatted, even tried to cook a spud over a small fire, but it wasn't successful.

Once when out walking to Wardown Park to collect gloriously shiny, deep brown conkers I happened to ask John who his best friend was. He replied: 'You know who.' It was such a sophisticated and direct response that I never forgot it. He was my first and best friend, probably the only 'best friend' I ever had.

One day I was invited to his birthday party, just across the road where he and Janet lived. Ma said: 'You can't go like that' as I was about to leave in my usual scruffy street clothes. For some reason I remember her command that I dress up – I didn't realise that it was important as a sign of respect for the neighbours and a birthday was a big deal for a kid, yet no party was ever made for me, not one. My sister had one each year. I don't know why and I never knew why – in fact, it didn't really affect me all that much since not getting anything I wanted was becoming awfully familiar. Since then birthday parties have always been anathema to me, even arranging a rare party takes some overcoming of resistance.

It didn't bother me that Beryl had her party each year when all her friends would gather in the empty front room. She was older than me, so somehow deserved it; she also had a tennis racket and played tennis in the park. I had my swimming, but I did fancy a bike very badly. Indeed, I begged for one with a passion that almost consumed me and would have melted the heart of a dragon, but it was denied me: 'Too dangerous – you'll have an accident' and even, God forbid, 'We're going to America'.

Then one day Dad made a pact with me, somehow adopting the role of Mephistopheles. He promised me that if I would be on best behaviour for 40 days then he would buy me my cherished bike. (I'm sure he was unaware of the biblical resonance of that number – Christ's 40-day fast in the desert, and when it rained on Noah's Ark for 40 days and 40 nights). As far as I was concerned, this was a pact made in blood. It seemed a good deal so I was determined to be on my absolute best behaviour: never arguing, eating whatever slop was put in front of me, going to bed when I was told. Despite the strains and twitches this caused me, through the mist I could see my bike at the end of it. It was on the 25th day or so that I had a really minor eruption and for a moment lost sight of the dream, but for this offence Dad sentenced me to start the 40 days all over again from day one! But begin again I did, biting my tongue, gritting my teeth and lo and behold, the 40 days passed.

It was the longest 40 days of my life and in the end... no bike. (A few years later, even though I really could have bought myself one by then, I actually did the despicable and stole one – I had no feeling for another's loss.) Meanwhile, I had been betrayed, as I would be time and time again by this really peculiar bloke. I never forgot his act of betrayal and I believe it may have manifested itself in later years when I would suffer extraordinary pangs of guilt whenever I treated myself to something. Sometimes the guilt would torment me so much that I would have to return my beloved object to the store: I would feel great relief if they were able to take it back, even if I had to endure them knocking off 20 or 30 per cent since they claimed it was no longer new, though of course they would still sell it as such. Those 40 days had a lot to do with it, I think.

One day I was playing in the garden in Luton when I heard Dad proudly shout through the window as he had just returned from one of his many excursions to London. I thought I heard him say 'Bicycle!' and so I rushed in, my spirits on fire. But I had misheard him in my wish fulfillment for he had merely uttered 'Beigels!' Somehow he thought that would thrill me, yet it didn't. Gradually I grew wary of the strange beast, my father. He never really fathered me but was fond of giving advice, which was usually of a negative nature. So those twin occupations in my mind, the piano and the bike, were denied me and in the trough left in my mind by the absence of those treasures, there developed the two-headed beast of fear and loathing.

One day he did bring me a cheap watch since I had been begging for one for some time, although that was much lower on the list of my priorities. But the watch had no second hand and I badly wanted that, so I had the temerity to refuse it. To my surprise he didn't rant and rave, but took it back. A day or two later, he came back with a watch… with a second hand. Perhaps he was trying to compensate for the bike.

Since that time, however, I mostly wear a cheap digital watch and although I have bought myself a more expensive piece, I seldom wear it. I have injected my dad into me and he is always saying, 'No, no, no!' so now I find myself saying it for him! Sometimes I get a mild pang when I see a colleague wearing an expensive watch: in my flawed interpretation, I feel they must have been more deserving of theirs, even stronger. But I have found ways of getting over it – if I do buy something it has to be morally worthwhile, like a painting, and I have a few of those. But I don't take things back anymore: I just sit on them and sweat it out.

Now my mother took it upon herself to be my 'moral' guardian and took me to a school with twice-weekly Hebrew lessons for us little yiddles, which would also help familiarise ourselves with our great and fascinating history. Now I became aware of my ethnic roots and since it was a normal school during the day, classes were always held in the evening or on Sunday mornings. We were given these strange characters to learn, which I found strangely compelling. Soon I was able to learn the alphabet and read words without a clue as to their meaning. For some reason the teacher was so obsessed with us learning to read that he always forgot to tell us what we were reading, but it didn't matter since we all droned on without rhyme or reason.

Sometimes a lovely and very gentle young Jewish woman would come in. She would tell us about the important events in the Old Testament and if there were few of us for this, she would gather us round her desk to tell the stories. I found her so sweetly compelling that on one occasion while she was telling us something or other, I found myself slowly stroking one of her hands, which was placed on the desk. This I did so spontaneously since she was so appealing to me. I clearly remember that incident: she briefly looked up but said nothing, accepting my childish caress for exactly what it was. But she didn't say 'Please don't do that' nor did she withdraw her hand as I gently caressed it. She was the first woman outside my mother or sister that I ever touched but I never touched either of them with the love I felt for my divine teacher!

While at the classes I loved the stories of our past: of Abraham and Isaac, Jacob, Joseph and his coat of many colours, the exodus from Egypt (most important), fast days and the solemnity of Yom Kippur, the Day of Atonement. Then there was New Year – dressing up in your best suit and going to the building that had been converted to a synagogue; and of course hearing, albeit from another source, of the massacre of the Jews in Europe. I had another friend in Luton's Highfield Road called Baxter, who always seemed to be informed about all sorts of things that never came my way. He told me if Hitler ever conquered Britain, all us Jews would be wiped out. It didn't bother me in the least since he was always the bearer of bizarre news. Besides since we, the British, were the 'good' guys, I knew the Nazis would never be able to step foot in our green and pleasant land unless they happened to be homegrown! I was sure he made a lot of it up, it seemed so far-fetched – in fact, this child Baxter knew more than anyone.

Life more or less continued as before with the occasional air raid siren, even in Luton since the town was a large industrial base. My life was simple, my needs minimal, although one day in the shop just opposite Maidenhall School I saw a magnificent toy fort. The tower could be detached and it had a drawbridge; it was the most beautiful thing I had ever seen and I craved it mightily. Later I saw Ma struggle down the street, carrying it in her arms and I was utterly overwhelmed with emotion for at last my wishes had been fulfilled. I leapt upon it, arranged all my soldiers inside and spent many a happy hour with it. I adored my fort and I kept it for years.

On rare occasions Ma and I would travel down to London, usually by 'Greenline' coaches, to visit our relatives in Myrdle Street, Stepney (off Commercial Road). Here lived Dad's sister Mary, her husband Uncle Henry and their two sons, Willie and Sid and one daughter, Kitty. At that time Kitty was a completely crazy pest, but she grew up to be a fine, warm-hearted woman.

The East End was a desolate landscape full of craters courtesy of German bombing raids, although when covered in snow in the winter, it actually looked very pretty. My cousin Sid (who was about my age or a year older) came to stay with us in Luton for a few days and I realised how modest and civilised I was through the influence of country life, compared to dear Sid. It was quite a shock to my sweet gentile friends, Janet and John: he was swift to argue and insult them as if it was part of the bonding ritual. I was amazed at his behaviour though I secretly admired him since I was a bit quiet and withdrawn.

One day Dad came home with a red Singer second-hand sports car but since it only had two seats, we were rarely able to enjoy it as a family. A strange choice for a man with two kids, perhaps. On the other hand, given his disposition, maybe not!

When we moved into Highfield Road, this dull, suburban street like a million others, we inherited a black cat called Peter. I grew to love this strange and exotic creature until one day Mrs Glazer (the woman who rented the house to us) came to pick up her cat, now that they were comfortably ensconced a few miles away, a fact that nobody thought to mention to me since I believed the cat came with the house. A few weeks later we heard a scratching at the window and lo and behold, our darling boy had returned, all the way from Dunstable, an incredible distance! This amazing animal had found his way back to his home (and us). We stared in awe and complete surprise and as soon as we let him in, he jumped on the kitchen cupboard and hauled down a large slab of fish intended for our supper. Of course we could only gaze in admiration at this gargantuan feat and that night, there was nothing that our beloved and heroic cat could not have had, we were so pleased to see him again. It must have been one of the happiest days of my life and maybe for this reason I have been attached to cats ever since.

It was at Maidenhall School that I must have acquired a taste for acting since once a week our divinely attractive teacher would read us the story of Brer Fox, that canny creature who was always deceiving Brer Bear. We would then get up and act it out. Each week the teacher (who, I believe, had a soft spot for me) invited me to play the main role – which I did with apparent glee and unselfconsciousness as I completely identified with the fox character. After a while I felt self-conscious about being singled out and that I should let another boy have a go at the lovely fox and so when as usual she asked me, I said this time I would play the bear. I remember she looked at me quizzically. For some reason it was the last time we did the story. Maybe she thought I was getting tired after a long run…

The other story that was read out to us was Rudyard Kipling's *The Animal Book* and I remember a character called

Riki-Tiki-Tavi. How could I ever forget the wild and intrepid beast? Just hearing those tales would hurl me into a completely different world.

Ma loved the movies and so once a week we would go to see a film and I recall being deeply impressed by *King Kong* and *Sinbad the Sailor* and very excited by Olivier's *Henry V*. Such was the degree of normality and security that at eight or nine years old I was allowed during the long summer to go about the town unaccompanied and visit the cinema alone. If the film had an 'adult' certificate (over-16s unless accompanied by an adult), I would stand outside and ask a grown-up to take me in! They were mostly housewives with their afternoons free. Even though I was lucky not to be molested by some paedophile, I think my mother was a trifle lax.

The war was over in May 1945 when I was seven years old. I clearly remember the street party and all the jolly festivities. Our ration books continued for a long time after the war but Dad was for some reason always able to buy chocolate from the spivs on the black market – which meant you spent an absolute fortune on a bar of chocolate but it tasted heavenly since it was so scarce. We were all reasonably content and life carried on much as before. For the occasional treat, Ma would take Beryl and me to her best friend Dinah, who lived in Edgware. Dinah and Sid Katz, her husband, were delightful, warm-hearted people who knew

Ma as a child from the East End before the war. She now had this beautiful, warm homely house in Edgware and I could never imagine her living in the filthy old East End.

Part of the adventure was the freedom: Dinah always allowed us to wander round the house at will and to play the piano in her front room. For some bizarre reason I continued to harbour this obsession and would miserably tinker away at the same six opening notes for the 'Warsaw Concerto', over and over again. Still the penny didn't drop. Now this is curious because Ma played the piano as a child and was in fact considered a bit of a prodigy and played for her school. Like me, she had begged for a piano as a child but this was different since Ma was the last of 11 children and so she had many 'Mas' and 'Pas', who were her older siblings, and her boxing brother Alf Hyman bought the piano for her.

Alf was, of course, a bit of a hero in Batty Street, just off Commercial Road, where Ma lived. At least once a week he would go to the local boxing arena in Aldgate, where he soon acquired a sterling reputation as one of the best two-fisted fighters in the business. After the devastating fight with flyweight legend Jimmy Wilde, however, he was so badly beaten that it really put paid to his career. In his heyday he would beat nearly everyone and was characteristically generous with his modest purses. After he paid for his little sister's piano, she practised like mad and was soon proudly giving small public performances at school. According to

27

Ma (and I have no reason to disbelieve her), her father eventually sold the piano when she turned 15 since he felt it was high time that his daughter went to work. Maybe that explains everything.

Anyway, Dinah had a smart son who was just a few years older than me. Alan was a very bright boy, who was chic and handsome. He showed me around the area, which was full of little woods and creeks and also introduced me to the more refined arts of hairdressing and Brylcreem, explaining how if you put it on your hair then you could push it up into a wave – wonderful for my untamed mop! I believe he was an apprentice hairdresser (it was a very popular occupation for Jews for some reason, which no doubt goes back centuries). Naturally I was so intrigued by this discovery that from then on, I would apply the magic white cream to my hair and slowly push it up into the required height, although Ma was not so keen on this or the subsequent defiling of her nice white pillows. At Dinah's the food was always tasty and in fact more edible and less stinky than at Ma's. For much of my young life I was a vegetarian since I just could not stand the stench of garlic and onions, but one day Dinah fried some nice lean bits of steak and I suddenly found it absolutely delicious. From then on, I overcame my distaste for meat.

As I grew older these lovely people seemed sadly to vanish from my life and even Ma's life too, but in the early post-war years then we did see a lot of them. One day Ma told me that 'Aunty Dinah' was coming to Luton to visit us and so I ran from school in high expectation. When I rushed into the living room and didn't see her, naturally I asked: 'Where is she?' Ma replied that unfortunately she couldn't make it that day, which caused me to explode into howls and tears, whereupon Dinah magically appeared from under the table whence she had been hiding for a tease.

A few minutes later we heard Beryl coming in and so Dinah hid again and did the same trick. As Beryl came in, she also asked, 'Where is Dinah?' Now Beryl was seven years older than me and of course far more in control of her feelings, but even so I was totally shocked at her reaction. There seemed to be nothing except a mild disappointment and I wondered how on earth she didn't break down and burst into tears as I had done. Of course I couldn't know that at this time growing enables you to control these emotions although I can't say it's had too much effect on me!

Now that the war was over we were able to travel and get around a bit. One day Dad rented a car to take us all on a trip to Brighton and as it drew past the pavilion, I was gob-smacked at my first glance of the deep blue sea; it was also a perfect summer's day. We were booked into a pleasant, cheap-and-cheerful B&B and the landlords, a young woman and her husband, looked after us really well – so much so that we all wanted to stay a few more days while Dad went back to Luton since he probably had to work (you never knew with him). We walked everywhere in an idyllic post-war Brighton, played 'housy-housy' on the pier and took the miniature Volk's railway to Black Rock swimming pool. It was a marvellous lido and this was a blissful time in a typical English summer. (Just above Black Rock is the so-elegant Lewes Crescent, where 40 years hence I would be sitting on my own balcony, watching the sunset from the first-floor flat of a splendid Regency house.)

Each year for maybe three years we returned to that lovely little guesthouse where they were so warm and friendly and where the landlady greeted Ma like a loving sister and Ma even used to help around the house! The next time we went there, I don't recall Dad being around.

But at home I always remember the horrid rows that were conducted in a language so alien to my ears it might have been forged in hell. Since it was in Yiddish I had no idea what was going on, but while I was ignorant of the language no one could ignore the acidity of those bloodcurdling curses. I got to learn the horrid words, all to do apparently with inflicting terrifying illness and curse in your guts.

Ma's dream of joining the rest of her family in New York never left her since all of her brothers and sisters had, along with thousands of others, abandoned the dark recesses of the East End. Obviously we had to wait for the war to be over, which is why all my desperate wishes were denied since it was always the same refrain: 'Next year in America…' But one day it did happen and this time I was told well in advance as a caution. Ma said we were going to try it out for three months and that was what I was expected to tell my teacher at school, though why I should have to impart this information when it was a parent's duty is merely indicative of just how careless they both were about my welfare and even my mental state. But I did as I was told, then said goodbye to John and Janet. Off to Southampton we went to sail on the *Queen Elizabeth*, then the largest liner in the world. Our trunks proudly displayed the big red Cunard Line labels, complete with cabin number and name.

Dad rented a car to take us to Southampton only he was not going with us, can you believe it? He was coming after, so as 'to tidy things up'. Blah, blah, blah… With this strange bloke, you couldn't make it up and Ma so sweetly believed everything, but really, I think, she was afraid not to. As we entered the docks at Southampton all I could see was this huge wall in front of me until I realised it was actually the side of that enormous ship: the first and original *Queen Elizabeth*. It was astonishing! We embarked with all the formalities and were shown to our cabin. Ma and I were sharing a windowless two-bunk inner cabin, while Beryl was sharing with another passenger. Everything was wonderful and dizzying; I loved the constant smell of polish, food, wood, oil and the tangy scent of the sea. It was unforgettable, and I dived into the labyrinthine tunnels of the ship for most of the week. What an amazing experience for a child of 10 – nothing, but nothing, would ever be the same again.

Since it was October the weather was none too treacherous and I didn't suffer greatly from seasickness and spent most of my time exploring this great leviathan, usually ending up in the pool – which I'd sneak into since it was only in First Class. It was a small salt-water pool and the attendant assumed I was from First Class since I went everywhere quite boldly, never knowing I was a third-class citizen and that such pleasures were not meant for peasants from the lower strata. We were all deliriously happy on our floating hotel, being waited on hand and foot with n'ere a care in the world; there was always so much to see and do. In the afternoon I'd play deck 'quoits' (I believe it was called). In the evening we all gathered for dinner in the large lounge and our steward was a tough burly guy who used to entertain us with his cockney stories, but for a showstopper he would smash his fist into one of the large wooden columns. It appeared never to hurt him since he told us if you punch it in a certain way it doesn't cause any pain.

Early one morning we arrived in New York at dawn and the city was bathed in a dark gloomy mist. We could barely sleep anyway the night before and had all gathered on the deck to see the glittering skyline come into view. To say that I had never even begun to imagine anything like it could hardly convey my emotions at this incredible sight since the ship docked at Pier 93, where a whole nest of skyscrapers in Manhattan's financial district leapt up into view. As phenomenal as I had expected (and more), it was cataclysmic, almost unbelievable as if I was in a dream. Soon enough it grew light and we were all packed up and ready to go, but of course it took many hours before we could disembark since we were just steerage. Sometime in a very cool afternoon we did just that and waiting for us were Ma's sister Doris and her husband Sol. After all the hugging and weeping and kissing and laughter, since they had not seen each other in nearly 20 years, we all got in the car – a large Yankee limo. As I sat there in wonderment at it all, my aunt handed me a Hershey bar. And this was my first bite on American shores and it tasted truly wonderful.

We drove to the Bronx, giving me just a sidelong glance at the great metropolis. But then the buildings grew smaller and smaller until we arrived. Then a very Jewish area, it is now predominantly black. They set out a feast for us beyond compare but even with my huge appetite, it was too much for an English stomach conditioned by years of rationing. After a great wodge of strawberry ice cream, I was thoroughly sick! Uncle Sol entertained us royally with jokes and tricks since he was part of a Magic Circle. It's curious how so many Jews, like Houdini, David Copperfield and Uri

Geller, are quite devoted to magicians as if we wish to escape from this often less-than-generous world and into another one. And I myself have a particular penchant for magic in all its forms and only wish I could do it...

After staying the night, the next day we were picked up by my cousin Morris, my favourite cousin – oh, how happy I was to see him again – and taken to Ma's other sister Ray, who lived in Nyack, New Jersey. We soon arrived at this small, but typically American white-framed house in a charming old town straight out of a Norman Rockwell cover for the *New Yorker*. Great mansions lined the streets, with sumptuous lawns spread around them and even though Aunty Ray's was much smaller it still had that Old World charm. This was real America: everything smelled as America should smell, with that special odour of cheap cologne, candy and packaging.

I had to share the front room with Morris since he obviously gave up his room to Ma, so it must have been just a three-bedroom house. Unlike Ma, Aunty Ray was a tad authoritarian and wasn't having this once-a-week bath nonsense but the Yankee once-a-day model. I was so glad to see Morris again since he was such a kind, genial soul when he visited us in Luton. He owned a drugstore in the main street of Nyack and was something of a pillar of the society. As you entered the store, a small snack counter on the left (mandatory for all drugstores in those days) greeted you. Of course nothing pleased me more than to sit on a high stool at the counter and order my toasted cheese and salad with mayo. Pure bliss, and served by some charming black ladies, who were in fact the first black faces I had ever seen!

Apart from magazines, I had never seen a black person in the flesh or spoken to 'coloureds', as they were then called. It all seemed quite normal, even taken for granted, in this weird and wonderful new world in which I found myself. I'd then fill in the day with helping out, clearing things up, sometimes even selling the odd item. I don't think I became indispensable to Morris, but for a child there was always something to do or somewhere to go. Whereas for my mother… What could the poor woman do with herself all day long except wait?

I still wore my English suit with its short pants, so Morris took me to the elegant clothes shop next door and had me totally outfitted in not one but two suits with long pants, a top coat and a trilby, would you believe? Thus I went through a complete transformation: I was turned into a Yank and I loved it. I felt so gloriously grown up. The thrill of this transformation stayed with me each morning when I slid into my svelte long pants and felt the cloth wrapping itself round my legs, a reminder that all of a sudden I had been plunged into the adult world. Never again would I wear those miserable British short pants! I was truly a grown-up, an adult American and nothing in the world made me prouder.

My few days in Nyack were as content as any I can remember and the mood was reflected in a gentle fall that bathed the town in gorgeous rustic colours. Each morning, Aunty Ray poured me a large glass of ice-cold milk – another first since we never had a fridge before and I hadn't tasted anything so deliciously cold, although it was quite a shock at first. Then I'd climb into Morris's big car and he'd slowly drive into town for my day at the store. Like all, or most American families in those days, after dinner in the evenings we'd sit in front of the TV (a small black-and-white) and watch whatever was on. It was still the early days of television and so the signal would start with a picture of the Empire State Building and then it would begin.

But the idyll was not to last: time to get settled into the city and so we all got into the car and drove back to the Bronx, where Ma's other brother Joe had a large rundown rooming house on East 173rd Street. That house would have been a perfect double for the one in the *Psycho* movie. It was a strange old building from Victorian times, with warrens of rooms on each floor that Joe let to all manner of working-class men and women.

Uncle Joe was a tough old nut: he had spent years in New York (as a longshoremen, among other things) and he had invested his savings in this odd house. Joe showed us up to the flat in the attic that Ma, Beryl and me would occupy. We crawled up several flights of stairs, but as we came to the last set we found them so narrow that Ma and Beryl burst into hysterical laughter, which was in fact halfway to crying. Like all attics, it was a large area from front to back, but this wasn't just for us, oh no – the space was divided by a curtain since the front part was occupied by a simple-minded guy called Chris, who was a hospital janitor. There was a small stove on the landing and a toilet, but no bath: for that, we would go downstairs. To describe Ma's reaction as shocked would be an understatement. She was in a state of complete and utter depression: we had one room, one double bed and a single for me, with a small window at the end. And that is what Ma's relatives had found for us – it did not even make sense. But to me, it was heaven! I was in America.

In fairness to Ma's folks, they probably only wanted us to have somewhere to rest our heads for a few weeks until we found a nice cheap flat in the nearby Bronx and could then begin to live, work, attend school, go to movies, make friends and be just like anyone else and be happy in America. After all, Europe was virtually a dead zone and what a fantastic opportunity to start life over again. Unfortunately, one element was missing in all this: a father, husband and worker. With no job and little funds, Ma was just waiting for the big slob to get his arse over there. She was missing him badly, as I was to see in her mournful letters that I discovered years later. He was apparently winding up his 'affairs' and saving a little more money. The old bum was never short of a line to spin to Ma, which she of course swallowed. For me, life was normal and yet adventurous at the same time since I was attending school and my sister found a job as a counter hand in a small Jewish deli, which she really loved, but for Ma just waiting around was the beginning of a nightmare.

I can never forget Ma waving to me from the attic window as I went to school at P.S. 70 each morning and I remember it made me feel sad just to see her up there, as if locked away.

After school we spent much of our time in Uncle Joe's large front room – sitting, talking and playing the record player. There was one record that seemed to click with me and I'd play it over and over again: it was 'Peg O' My Heart'. Joe taught me how to use the phone and what to say and that was the first time I had a phone in my hands. When Ma first took me to the school for my interview I was astounded to see a cop in the building with a gun in his holster: P.S. 70 was a mixed school with a vengeance and I loved it.

Now I was slowly becoming an American. As a young English boy I was unique in class since they all believed I came from a war-torn London, where we were all starving and without a shirt on our back. Naturally, I didn't try to change their misconception about me. Our very charming teacher, Mr Rich, told the class one day how awful things were for us Brits and I felt a little queasy about being seen as a pathetic refugee. Arriving at school, we all marched to the large gym where in order to bind us in unity we'd sing the American anthem and take an oath of allegiance to the flag. Hey, we never did this in Maidenhall School! There, we'd sing 'All things bright and beautiful, all creatures great and small...' We'd then sing a song that I have never forgotten: it was composed by a Japanese woman so happy to have escaped her blasted nation that she composed a hymn to America, which started off quite stridently: 'I love life and I want to live...' It was quite emotional – somehow just to be in America pulled out all sorts of emotional commitments from you.

After this, we repaired to the gym to do a half-hour's workout, all in a sequence. We'd start with some running and then some pull-ups at the bar (which I quite liked) and then some passing of the oval-shaped football. Fortified in mind and body, we returned to our class – or so the theory goes.

In those days it was the fashion for kids to emulate adults and so girls would come to school wearing stockings and suspenders, lipstick and even nail varnish. It was a late-forties' post-war thing but still quite weird to see 11-year-olds hoisting up their stockings under the desk. We had a friendly, benign teacher in Mr Rich and of course the whole class burst into peals of laughter when I addressed him as 'Sir' and not 'Mr Rich' – I never made that mistake again. However, since their curriculum was nearly two years behind our far-superior education in England, I had the chance again to deal with those mysteries of mathematics, like algebra and geometry.

Across the road on 174th Street, now sadly ripped out to make space for a freeway, was a group of very simple shops and small cafes, plus tiny craft stores like cobblers, hairdressers and jewellers. This was my main social area to explore and right at the bottom end near the subway was a branch of the famous Nathan's deli, where I was introduced to one of the most extraordinary tastes of my life: a hot dog with sauerkraut and mustard. Nothing I had yet tasted in my life could compare to that strange, zingy flavour of the 'kosher hot dog', as they were called and the hamburgers were even better. On those long, grey wintry Sundays I was often sent out specially to pick up some burgers.

In the evening we'd sit with Uncle Joe, his bizarre wife Nancy (whose silver-blonde hair was piled up like a helmet) and their lovely daughter Sandra (whose head was also piled up, but with thick red hair). I rather liked Sandra. Those were all the adorable misfits of the Jewish race: bizarre and colourful, neither fish nor fowl, neither fully American nor Russian, Jewish but indifferent to it, a mishmash of the great American Dream. Joe also looked after my cousin Paula, who was the daughter of Ma's boxer brother, Uncle Alf. Lively Paula would always entertain us by doing the splits and handstands and was obviously destined for showbiz.

Sunday was our great 'treat' when Morris and Aunty Ray would pick us up for a day in Manhattan, where we would drive about. He liked to show us the 'sights', like The Bowery, where we saw dozens, if nor scores of 'bums', laying flat out in the street. At first I thought they were dead until Morris enlightened me that they were all dead drunk! Then we'd do a slow cruise through Central Park and end up with a Chinese meal. After our allotted time was up, Ray would remind Morris that they had to get back for a popular TV show that she didn't want to miss and then we were dumped back in l73rd Street for an early night. Ma was crying a lot by then and it was a sad sight; I didn't like what was happening to her but there was nothing that I could do except wait for the geezer she married to come and rescue her.

It so happened that one day in my usual solitary window-shopping along 174th Street I popped into a tiny jewellery store that sold mainly nick-nacks such as earrings, neck-laces and cheap watches since I wanted to upgrade my watch by having one of those fancy steel-stretch bands. So I went in and the youngish man sold me a stretch-metal band for a dollar and even attached it for me. We got talking and he was so friendly, so keen to hear my tale that I think I told him the story of my life and he invited me to pop in for a chat anytime I liked. At last I had a friend! I found this an immediate comfort since having no father in the social sense of the word and never having had the smallest chat with

41

him in my life, I had always been drawn to male adults many years older than me who would give me the time of day. So he was my first and true American friend and many happy moments I spent in his little oasis of tranquility. Before I left New York, months later, he made me a present of a small, gold-plated penknife that I cherished until I accidentally dropped it down a grate when we returned to a derelict East End. He was a good-hearted man and I really missed him.

As a child of 10 one doesn't need too much – just a bed, some food and somewhere to go during the day, like a decent school and the rest falls into place. Friends will soon materialise and what better place for all this to happen than in America? You possess nothing but your dreams and your abundant energy, but for a middle-aged woman whose life depends so much on her family and her husband, in the balance between desperation and hope, it's not so good. She has no home to call her own, not even a small flat, no social life, no job, little money and a family rapidly becoming disenchanted with her needs and wondering where on earth is the captain of the ship, who will guide us all on a straight course.

Well, the day had come when Dad eventually arrived. It took about two months for him to get his act together. I recall being put into one of the lodger's spare rooms – so he could have some time with Ma, I expect. I don't think Dad was too impressed with how little effort our relatives had made to try and find us a decent place to live. One night I felt either lonely or abandoned, I didn't know where I was anymore; I suffered a terrible nightmare and awoke howling. It was my sweet cousin Paula who rushed into my room to hold and comfort me.

Well, eventually Dad came, but he didn't seem to make much effort to either find work or an apartment for us. On the one night when we all went out for a drive round the Bronx, I can recall him saying, 'Oh how it's all changed, it's now like Broadway!' since a few neon lights had given the area a new sheen. I remember feeling even a little bit proud as he said that as if everything would now fall into place because he, Dad, was back at the helm.

I had my school each day and saw little of him until the evenings, when I would see him sitting in the front room with Uncle Joe, playing cards, smoking and doing all those grown-up things. Children are lucky, their lives are taken care of, but for adults it's not so easy: you have to take care of others and to be fair, that's what he did up till then. But suddenly he just seemed to give up, as if the struggle was too arduous in his middle age. Without more ado he packed up his bags and left. He deserted us, his wife and two children – tired of us and fled, didn't even bother to say goodbye to me… Nothing. Ma just said he had to go back. To tell the truth I barely even noticed him there and didn't miss him when he left. I never really found out what was at the bottom of that decision just to abandon us like that or how he had the heart to do it, but we continued as before.

Of course things had changed and Ma was gradually getting worse. Quite often to cheer her up, I would run down to Nathan's for a couple of burgers for us and run all the way back so they'd still be warm after I clambered up the stairs to our attic home.

Christmas came and we actually visited some distant relatives on Long Island: it was all white and cosy, very nice, but then New Year came and nobody invited us anywhere. After supper with Uncle Joe, we all went to bed early. We just lay there until there was a knock on the door and it was a friend of Beryl's from work, who was shocked to find us all tucked away like hermits in our little attic room. She was such a charming, lively young woman and she said: 'Hey, it's New Year's Eve, you can't just stay in!' And so this enterprising woman made us all get up and get dressed. She took us to the local diner: suddenly we were so happy; she saved our souls that miserable night. So it seemed that really one could do without Dad so long as friends rally round (and you, of course, round them).

Chris, the janitor living opposite behind the curtains, was also maybe feeling a bit sorry for us and offered to take us to the movies. He was a simple-minded but well-meaning guy, who I always had to remind to shut the bathroom door when taking a piss! However, he did take us out to the local movie house to see *The Invisible Man*. Before the film they even had a live act, which was unexpected and fun. At his suggestion I sat in the middle between him and Ma, so that Ma wouldn't feel uncomfortable.

As the nights were drawing in, often we just stayed upstairs to listen to the radio, which was always full of fun, silly things. My favourite programme was called 'The Creaking Door', which had a chill thriller broadcast every week and they were really first-rate. It always started with a deep voice announcing, 'This is the Creaking Door...' in sepulchral tones and then you'd hear the sound of a door slowly opening with a long, menacing creak to put you in the mood. The radio was on most of the day but it was the ads that never stopped, that crawled into your mind, like the toothpaste ad – 'You'll wonder where the yellow went when you brush your teeth with Pepsodent... Pepsodent... Pepsodent!'

With no home, no security, no husband and no work, Ma was in limbo. She had not worked since her teenage years as she had dedicated her life to looking after us so had probably lost confidence. Meanwhile, Beryl was getting on fine and enjoyed her job and was making friends, but Ma didn't even have a decent place to cook a meal. One day she just couldn't take anymore, so she said we were going to Nyack for a few days. She pulled me out of school and back to Nyack we went, but the mood of our relatives seemed to match the weather and we weren't made to feel welcome there, either by Ray and her bachelor son, Morris. Obviously they had a pleasant routine that they didn't wish to be turned upside down by needy, sad relatives and an ever-crying Ma.

So, one day, Ma then decided she could stand no more of it and so she booked us to return home in late January. It was the worst time of year when the snow was deeper than it had been for decades in New York. To her credit Beryl refused to go and so she stayed on. She loved America and had made lots of friends since she was a fairly outgoing person; even I had one or two as well. I certainly wasn't happy to go, but Ma had booked our return on the *Queen Mary*, the world's second-largest ship. It all happened rather too quickly for my taste but when you're a child you just go with the flow and so I did. There was little traffic on the streets that night since the snow was so thick that in the end we had to bribe a yellow cab to take us to the docks, where we embarked on the original *Queen Mary*. So this was farewell to New York.

I think a lot of theatres had to close on account of the record snowfall – even *A Streetcar Named Desire* with Marlon Brando, which was playing at the Barrymore (a theatre I was to occupy just 40 years later). Once on board, I did my usual routine and explored and raced around the ship, but I was glad to see Ma was better. She was back to normality, she was being looked after, people were friendly and she had good communication with others at the dining table but soon as I got on high seas I was sick as a dog. It was a ferocious crossing, as if even the high seas had it in for us. I was so ill that I was confined to the sick bay for three days and missed all the treats. After a few days I was feeling a little better and getting accustomed to the giant rocking horse so I got up and joined Ma for dinner. It was such relief to breathe in the air of freedom after that attic.

The ship provided entertainments each night even for the tourist class and after dinner we played 'housy-housy', which is really another name for bingo. To my great excitement I actually won. Not a fortune, I might add, maybe something in the region of £5, but it seemed like a fortune to me. Now to my great astonishment the compère got up to say the prize was to be given by the famous movie star and champion ice skater 'Belita'. In fact, by the most amazing coincidence I had just seen Belita in *The Gangster*, a movie that Ma and I watched on 42nd Street on one of our excursions onto the Great White Way. Here she was as large as life and giving me my prize... Oh, we were flying again! Oh, we were happy again, soaring into those majestic clouds called happiness.

I imagine she was asked to do this little duty as an honour to us in steerage, or is it just possible she was actually travelling in Third Class? Anyway, she lit up the entire room like a beacon. Naturally, I spoke to her and told her what I was doing and briefly what had happened while Ma sat beaming in the background. Belita warmed to me and of course, I immediately fell in love with her: she was divine. Beautiful, warm-hearted, she took to me since I was so enthusiastic about her and unbelievably had recently seen her movie, which had just opened in New York. I even remember saying you don't find many movie stars in Third Class, to which she replied: 'I'm just slumming', which I thought was an awfully smart thing to say (it was the first time I had ever heard that expression). Before she left, I asked if I could write to her and she said of course I might and wrote down her address in Beverly Hills. Then she got up, shook my hand, smiled and walked out of the room. Oh, some magic had entered my life!

The ghastly day soon arrived when we reached Southampton. Oh, what a grim, sorry sight it was compared to my arrival in New York in the October of the year before! However, it was made less horrible by my introduction to Henry Ford II in his cabin. During my perambulations round the ship it had been my habit to ask the purser if there were any famous people on board and he always smiled and said he couldn't reveal that. But as it was the last day he told me the great Henry Ford II was on board and seeing that I was hardly a threat, gave me his stateroom number. And so without more ado I found it and gently knocked on his door. (For some reason I always felt I could trust adults and the more famous, the better. Perhaps I felt fame was bestowed on the generous and large of heart. Since Dad was no longer a friend or mentor, I felt free to find surrogates wherever I chose.)

The door was opened by the great man himself and I was invited in. Children are no threat to adults and can so easily go on paths their elders fear to tread. Well, straightaway we were chatting and I was telling him and his nice wife my story, which they seemed to be quite taken by, although I never did elaborate or play for sympathy – it was just straightforward. Ford was a young man whom I believe had just taken over the great behemoth of the family empire. I simply sat on the bed and rapped away while they were finishing off their packing and getting ready to disembark. We must have docked since suddenly the room was full of reporters asking him questions about this and that, taking the odd picture and at one point looking at me. A reporter asked him: 'Is he your son?' The words stunned me and I swelled with pride. For a moment nothing on this earth would have been more wonderful than to be scooped up and taken away by Henry Ford II – I was never so proud. But then it was over and I left his cabin. The door closed, but I had been given my glimpse of heaven and went back to Ma. Dad was at the quayside waiting and he took Ma in his arms and gave her a big sloppy kiss, which I had never ever seen him do before, so he must have been trying to make amends for his horrible desertion of us all.

We got on the train to Victoria but even here he embarrassed us: when the ticket inspector came round, he said we were travelling in First Class with third-class tickets. Dad mumbled and fumbled, but for some reason the inspector allowed us to stay. We were now being taken under the wing of Dad's side of the family and he had arranged for us to stay with his brother (my Uncle Sam) in Cannon Street Road, Stepney. At Victoria station his wife, my Aunty Betty, was there to meet us. We all piled into a cab to the East End. Betty was friendly in the cab and even said 'He's got a bit of an accent', which was highly unlikely. Soon we were ensconced in Sam and Betty's flat on the top floor.

Dad, as usual, went off since there was no room for him although I never knew where he went and never asked. I slipped into bed with my cousin Barry, who was about a year younger than me. And that was that. Betty's words stuck in my mind about my accent. Yes, I had slowly been turning into an American when suddenly I was pulled out of that nourishing soil and returned to the land of damp, squalor and ration books.

Winter 1948

2008: I would be staging *On the Waterfront* at the Edinburgh Festival prior to the West End.

1998: I would be doing my one-man show *Shakespeare's Villains* at the Theatre Royal, Haymarket.

1988: I would direct Roman Polanski in Paris in my version of Kafka's *Metamorphosis*, as well as *Salome* in Dublin and *Coriolanus* in New York.

1978: I would be doing my play *East* in London's West End.

1968: I first staged *Metamorphosis* at LAMDA.

1958: I stepped into the Webber Douglas School of Singing and Dramatic Art in South Kensington.

1948: It was the heaviest snow of the century and even the bombed-out cesspits of the East End were transformed into a crystal fairyland.

———⪼◆⪻———

Ma immediately enrolled me at Christian Street School, the same school she had attended some 40 years earlier. I would be there for a year before sitting what they then called the '11 Plus' to decide whether my life would be blighted by a second-rate education or uplifted by grammar school. Despite the recent months of chaos, I passed with flying colours. On the first day at school I seem to have shocked all the kids since they had never seen anything like it: a 10-year-old wearing a smart, double-breasted suit with long pants. In their grubby short pants, with chafed knees, scraggy pull-overs and snotty noses they stood there, blinking with watery eyes and staring at me in sheer wonderment. I was the centre of attention, no doubt about it. To them I was a star!

Since Ma and I had no real home of our own, I stayed for school dinners – a miserable, drab affair. I sat there with the other kids and after tasting the rather bland food, asked for salt. They all looked at me and giggled at such audacity since nobody had ever asked for anything before – you just got your food and wolfed it down and that was that. Realising I was not yet institutionalised, the nice lady teacher actually got up and brought me a salt cellar from the staffroom. The kids must have thought I was a bit too fancy for their taste and thereafter called me 'Spiv' since that was what they thought I looked like. And that was the name they anointed me with and it is what I was called until I left that school. I got used to the place and it was a pleasant enough time except for one occasion when I was repeatedly punched in one ear by a pair of bullies, who for some reason took exception to me. Since I thought that this is the way of life I didn't even think of reporting it to anyone. I thought maybe I deserved it.

Every morning we assembled for the school tradition of hymns and prayer but for some reason this irked me. One morning I removed myself from the hall and sat in class until it was over. A few minutes later, one of the teachers came bounding in, demanding to know why I wasn't at morning prayer and I replied, a tad self-consciously, that I was Jewish and they were Christian prayers. He glared at me and replied: 'So what? I am Jewish too and we have all races at the school and these prayers are for everybody, so don't act so superior.' After that I never absconded from morning prayer again. Also, I learned a valuable lesson.

Our new home… Eventually after some to-ing and fro-ing we found a two-room flat, though you could hardly call it a flat – just two small rooms with a sink and a stove in the back room, an outside toilet and no bathroom, shared with a large, tough old grey cat, who belonged to the landlord upstairs. It was in Anthony Street, halfway up Commercial Road, E1. The toilet was quite an unpleasant experience on cold nights, but it was a friendly little street that probably hadn't changed much in a hundred years, built mainly to serve the teeming workforce of the East End in the 19th century. All the houses were identical, with basements that were hardly used any more since little light came into them. Most importantly, there was a small cinema in Commercial Road at the top of the street called the Palaseum, now sadly gone. It was a charming place and a source of my further education. Once a week without fail Ma and I would watch the latest offerings.

I was growing fast and was continually hungry, so Ma would make some sandwiches and bring a bottle of sugary Tizer with us and I would get through the lot. I recall seeing Ayne Rand's amazing *Fountainhead* with Gary Cooper, Patricia Neal and Raymond Massey, which impressed me so much that for some time my only ambition was to be an architect.

Next door to us was the Scopp family and little Sadie Scopp played the child parts in Yiddish at the Grand Palais, one of the last Yiddish theatres in London. So now we were at last back in the ghetto from whence we sprang, though in much-reduced circumstances. Dad's sister Mary lived a few streets away in Myrdle Street, just off Commercial Road and was married to Henry Bennet, who was a barber of sorts. Their two sons, Willie and Sydney, became part-time pals although Barry (Sam's son) and me were the only ones to go on to grammar school. For the next two years, Anthony Street became our home but it was not insufferable since everything was within easy reach.

Betts Street Baths, off Cable Street, had a pool as well as hot baths, where you could just sit in huge enamel tubs and shout for 'more hot water, number five, please!' since you couldn't control your own supply and of course I went swimming there nearly every day after school. This was one of my main joys and outlets and I made friends with the silver-haired pool attendant, who encouraged me one day to go for my mile certificate by swimming 73 lengths (which I duly did) and this was a source of great pride to both of us. Also, the benign man pressed a two-shilling piece, quite a fortune in those days, into my hand at the end. In the summer we had the beautiful, open-air Victoria Park lido, where I would also go most days even when it was raining just to get out of those two rooms since there was little else to do.

On the other side of the street lived an Irish family who had a son called Cornelius (who I called 'Conny'). We became good friends and spent a lot of time together. He introduced me to the beach by the Tower of London, where an enlightened council had wisely laid tons of sand. When the tide was out, it became the Costa Blanca for us East-Enders and we all threw ourselves into the river with abandon. Even Ma came a few times as you could hire deckchairs – she of course would never swim in that filthy cesspit of a river.

One of the most memorable times at Christian Street School was the last lesson on Friday afternoon when the adorable Miss Parry would read to us from *The Hound of the Baskervilles* by Sir Arthur Conan Doyle. This seemed to make a great impression on me for she read it so well and so convincingly that I was absolutely enrapt and at the same time learned of the enormous power of words and storytelling. In fact, we lived for words. We read, went to the library each week to take out our quota of books, listened to the radio on BBC every night and became hooked on the serials, especially the creepy ones read by Valentine Dyal – he was our fave. We loved *In Town Tonight*, with its unique opening when London stops and the traffic is heard coming to a standstill, while we learned about the special guest 'in town tonight' and the wonderful finish – 'Carry on, London!' – when the 'frozen' traffic suddenly came to life.

The corrupting influence of TV was in no way part of our culture, nor were there sleazy shock-jocks or slimy double-entendres, which is not to say it was puritanical either – it was just incredibly normal, innocent and highly informative.

For a special Sunday morning treat we might go to Rogg's Deli in Cannon Street Road and buy a few beigels and some thin slivers of smoked salmon (a king's ransom in those days). Ma would buy just a quarter of a pound and ask the man to throw in some skin (which of course was free) and then we'd go home. With some cream cheese smeared on the beigel and sliced pickled cucumber on top, we would feast. It would heighten whatever mood we might have: nothing mattered and the stale old East End faded into the background. Or we would shop in Hessel Street, a narrow tributary off Commercial Road and a market like no other on earth. Yiddish was spoken throughout the market, which seemed to specialise in poultry, for the shops with their sad, thin little kosher birds hanging up were everywhere, but also cheeses, beigels, pretzels and black bread and rye bread, olives, pickles and sprats, kippers, eggs, everything you might need. People would come from all over the world just to remind themselves of this remnant of their past but now this street has been destroyed, those wonderful old Dutch-style buildings torn down. It has vanished, almost as if it never existed and now it's another cold, dead road.

On hot summer days the East End was unbearable and so Ma and me (Beryl was not yet back from New York) would take the train from Liverpool Street station down to Southend and spend the day there. It was always an exciting experience but when the tide was out, no matter how far you walked you would never get further or deeper into the water than up to your knees and of course we would go on the train to the end of the pier. When we returned to our home in Anthony Street, we would find occupants of the entire street sitting outside on chairs to get some fresh air and gossip. I had never seen anything like it in my life and I know Ma hated walking the gauntlet till we got to our small house. Yet curiously enough, after a while she too would sit outside the house on a chair and sometimes go inside to make chips for the kids. I didn't much like this since I couldn't play on the street without her eyes always on me.

Ma continuously wrote to the council for re-housing and we were on the list, but the list was enormously long, not only because the bombing had decimated huge swathes of the East End but also through slum clearance, although the Labour government under Clement Attlee was building council flats at an enormous rate. Dad of course did nothing to help get us re-housed – I think he liked being back in a 'bachelor' life again and I didn't even know where he slept or what he did, but he did have a job as a tailor in a shop just up the road from us. Occasionally I would pop in to see him, though not that often. However, he seemed to be in a benign mood so not living with us obviously suited him and he blessed us with an occasional visit.

There seemed to be so many stray cats and kittens roaming around that I felt compelled to bring the odd needy one home to look after it. Some were so lively and they gave Ma such joy to see their antics that I took to bringing in more, and then one had six kittens so we had about eight cats. They were our friends, our children and little clowns, but even with looking after they seemed to perish before adulthood from the loathsome conditions in the house – I just hope it wasn't Ma's food!

Now the time had come for me to enrol at my grand new school, which was Raines Foundation in Arbour Square, a most elegant and established school for grammar-school boys:

> *A school providing a free education for poor children, established in 1719 by a devout Christian who made his fortune selling alcohol. It retained much of its history and traditions. It's motto – 'Come in and learn your duty to God and Man'.*
>
> Raines Foundation

Ma took me to Gardner's Corner at Aldgate to buy the requisite uniform of blazer, cap and tie. Then one September morning I turned up for my first day at grammar school. I was so very proud for now I could carry a case to put my schoolbooks in. This contributed to my sense of moving into adulthood for I had always seen it in movies, kids going home with a satchel full of books, especially American movies. On the very first day we all sat an exam designed to stream us into three groups: A, B and C. Happily, I was put into the 'A' group, which confirmed my sense of worth. That first day I was so deeply impressed by the ancient rituals – the singing in school assembly, the instruction of how to conduct yourself and what to say when you wanted to go to the toilet – *'Please sir, may I go forth?'* And at the day's end I expected some homework to thus fulfill my expectation of higher education. When this wasn't forth-coming, I shot my hand up and asked for some. The teacher seemed bemused: he looked at me, smiled and then asked the class if they would like some homework. Only a few hands shot up but he did give us something small to do, which pleased me no end since I was now a bona fide student.

Most of the teachers were civil and pleasant enough, particularly our English teacher, Mr Chivers, who always had a fine white handkerchief tucked inside his sleeve and a charming smile. For him I studied hard and was always near the top of his class. I also excelled in French since nothing was so exciting to me as learning another language. 'Top boy, very good work indeed' my first report said for my efforts in French. Unfortunately, the school, though very liberal and with high standards, still carried with it some dusty old disciplinary customs of a bygone age. It had a taste for cruelty – beatings, in particular – and one was punished for almost every trivial misdemeanor such as chatting in class, for which you would be given a 'pencil' entry, when your crime was recorded in a large book. After three pencil entries, you would be given the dreaded 'ink' entry and if you received three ink entries, you would face the humiliation of being thrashed in front of the whole class.

It would almost be impossible for a young boy not to receive the requisite amount of 'entries' for being merely a bit lively and so it was for me. I was asked to step out and bend down. As I remember, the gym master enforced the punishment with a vigour that was astonishing. The first whack took my breath away… I couldn't believe it and screamed out in pain. But then he asked me to bend down again. The second almost made me faint and I cried as I have never cried before. But still he told me to bend for the third, which he administered with an equal will as the other two. Returning to my seat, I wept shamelessly. I was left with three great weals on my backside that took weeks to fade. This was child cruelty of the highest order and I had done virtually nothing to warrant such punishment, but it began a suspicion verging on hatred for the adult world when I once had such trust – now I would know better.

Raines was a school dedicated to rugby and not the more common football, so each Wednesday we were all marched to the tube to traipse out to Hainault, where the school had a playing field and some tacky old changing rooms. I loathed it, especially on those freezing-cold winters and eventually found some medical excuse to get out of it and take the afternoon off. However, I did like the gym and found I had quite an aptitude for leapfrogging over the horse from the springboard, doing somersaults and handsprings. For lunch I avoided the school junk and would go to Joe Lyons teashop just down the road. Lyons was the workingman's teashop and there was nothing like it: thick tomato soup with a mashed potato squished in was a favourite.

But there was nothing in the world like Petticoat Lane for a Sunday morning's adventure. Across a vast network of roads, from Wentworth Street to Brick Lane, was a massive jumble of every item known to mankind and even animals at the Bethnal Green Road end. Of course you could not go past without wishing to fondle, hold and play with the puppies and kittens all desperately seeking some kind owner. Then the cigarette cards were so tempting – all those wonderful shiny packets of every card under the sun, from boxers to movie actors, jockeys, soldiers from all nations… Yet at school we flicked the poor cards against a wall and he whose card was nearest of course won all the others. And there was the area where they sold glorious stamps from every corner of the world – the smaller and poorer the country, the larger and more colourful the stamp, or so it seemed. Every week I religiously collected them until I had quite a magnificent album… until one day when I was about 12 and had a fervent desire to turn the stamps into cash, whereupon I sold them all at a ridiculously low price.

A whole Sunday morning down the Lane was an invitation to immerse oneself in the bizarre wonders of the world. It was a labyrinth of streets that I would never tire of navigating. During the week I would go to the Oxford and St George's Youth Club in Berners Street, where I could engage in any number of activities like ping pong, art classes, gym or just goof around – it didn't matter what, as long as you were off the street. How enlightened some people were in those dark, gloomy days of the East End when they set up centres and clubs for young people: now there is nothing, all gone. Now it's Blockbuster Video. Going to the Saturday-morning movies was a natural must and the huge Troxy Cinema was the East End choice. Fortunately that beautiful building still stands, even if its current use as a bingo hall is a tad diminishing to a once-great old building. One day it will spring to life again.

Each summer Ma thought it a good idea to send me off to the club's free summer camp for two weeks and so we'd all get on a big coach to some remote place. I did not care for that at all. It meant sharing a tent with the vilest bunch of East End louts that it was my misfortune to know. And I'm not being just superior: I just think the years in Luton 'civilised me' and I never acquired their brutalised street behaviour so for me it was not too much fun and I could not wait to get home. However, it was around this time that romance seeped into my heart. Deeply frustrated with the long summer in our endless twilight zone, one day Ma took us back to Luton to stay with a very nice family called the Bodinetz's, who were also exiled to Luton during the war but had stayed on. In fact, we knew them while we were there. I was never so glad as to be in their lovely home with clean sheets and fresh socks – Mum got so depressed that she sometimes forgot to wash my socks and so Mrs Bodinetz, who was so shocked at the state of them, did them for me.

By now it was a sweet, rolling summer and the days were spent playing cricket in the local park. Lionel, their son, with whom I bonded immediately, brought along a very pretty girl called Shirley. At this stage of my life I only saw her as another kid to play with and we had a lot of fun together, they were really happy days. Sadly all too soon the time came to go back home and I was waiting outside for the car to take us to the station. Lionel suddenly said to me: 'Shirley said you could kiss her goodbye, if you wish to…' She was waiting out of sight perhaps, waiting for that moment, but since it was so much in the open I was just too embarrassed by the sheer exposure. Of course I badly wanted to kiss her but somehow I couldn't. I couldn't even say goodbye to her and then we left.

There are certain loves you never forget: the image stays with you for a long time and forms something inside of you, like a knot in a tree. It never really fades and so it was with Shirley. Perhaps she became a template, something with which all others are compared. After a few days back in our 'beloved' Anthony Street, Ma told me that I had a letter from Shirley, a beautiful letter in her large clear hand-writing. I was amazed, even quite excited, to hear from her and of course I swiftly wrote back. She wrote simply about her life in Luton and how she was happy that we had met. I wrote back in a similar vein and this correspondence went on and on for over three years! All I could ever dream of was returning to Luton and seeing her again, but I wasn't sure how this could be done. How did you get the train or bus? Anyway, I couldn't do it alone – I hadn't the knowledge of how to do those things yet. So we wrote and each time I sent a letter, I looked forward to the reply and it was never long in coming.

There are some events in your life that are major steps, forever in some cases, in the shaping of who you'll be and going to America was one of those. It was the most dramatic and exciting event that a 10-year-old could possibly expe-rience. Attending grammar school was another and no one could have been prouder than me as I donned my school blazer with its distinctive blue shield badge for the first time. But Shirley somehow defined me emotionally as a fully charged young male who had the capability to form a relationship with a young female, a girl of my own age. To me, it seemed like heaven; it gave me someone to think about apart from myself, also a sense of belonging. How I looked forward to her letters.

Strolling along the Whitechapel 'Waste', an old market that appeared each Saturday along Whitechapel opposite the London Hospital, I was intrigued to see a small crowd surrounding a strange-looking man with a large hooked nose and fancy, greasy-black hair, who was enchanting the crowd with a sales pitch that was nothing less than hypnotic. He was merely selling ballpoint pens, still a bit of a novelty in those far-off days. Certainly he had the gift of the gab and after the crowd had bought some pens or simply drifted away, I looked at the multitude of different coloured pens and we got chatting. He confessed he needed someone to mind the stall while he went to Joe Lyons, just next to Whitechapel tube, for a cup of tea and would I do it? I was thunderstruck that someone would simply trust me just out of the blue like that, but he did and off he went. So I stood behind the stall and felt mighty important until he returned a few minutes later and before I knew it, I was the Pen King's assistant.

I'd never seen a performer like that before, someone who could excite the crowd with a simple pen, but that he did. Every so often he would start again with a great yell and the people would stop and then he'd throw the pens down onto a dish to show how resilient they were, how you could write for months before they ran out and when they did, you just bought a refill – all this delivered with humour, sarcasm and panache.

So every Saturday I would come down to the Waste and at the end of the day he would give me five shillings, which was pretty good wages then. After a few weeks I tried to do the 'pitch' but I didn't sound quite right and I could never get up that splendid courage to get out there and do it. He was also a part-time jazz singer, the kind who croaks out old Sinatra and Frankie Lane songs in East-End pubs and seedy clubs. Though an odd-looking guy with a pronounced limp who seemed to have everything against him, he had a real saucy tongue and I loved being on that stall and watching him.

We became really good mates and one day he took me to his home in Hornsey, north London, which he shared with his two elderly sisters. On hot days after work we'd go to the local outdoor pool. Now although I was just past 11 years old, I was well aware of men who liked young boys, but he never ever came onto me – he just liked my company as I liked his. I never tired of seeing him hypnotise the crowd and then I would take the pens, sell them and take the money, so I was his sorcerer's apprentice. Indeed, I loved the market life and all the zany characters around it, with their insane stories and filthy tongues.

I stayed with the Pen King for about a year but slowly drifted away once we all moved to a new council flat in Manor House, N4. In the meantime, my sister Beryl returned from America and quickly settled in. I don't think she ever wanted to return so Dad actually went over there and brought her back with him. This made the purchase of a 'put-u-up' necessary, which entailed unfolding the bloody thing at night and then folding it back up again in the morning, but we soon got used to it and even grew to quite like it. At least on Saturday mornings I could escape to the kids' shows at the Troxy Cinema on Commercial Road, near my school. The other cinemas were The Poplar, further up the Commercial Road (a little seedy) and one in Brick Lane, where Ma would pick me up after Hebrew classes. They took place in what used to be a great chapel, then a synagogue and now a mosque but in those days Brick Lane was a completely Jewish neighbourhood as was most of the East End, really. Ma took me to the movies a lot then since she didn't seem to have a husband to take her...

Woodberry Down Estate, Manor House, N4

When Woodberry Down was built in 1946–52, it was considered to be the estate of the future. You might call it Orwellian with its stark, brutalised architecture. Leaving the more normal and pleasant roads, with their houses with small front gardens and larger back ones in Amhurst Park, you suddenly entered a concrete zone that stretched out almost to infinity. It was conceived and designed basically for slum dwellers of the East End – of which of course, I was one. After the war, work began in earnest and nearly 2,000 flats were built, thus changing the whole character of the Borough and putting thousands of Labour-voters into a Conservative area.

⟨≡⟩◆⟨≡⟩

At last we were offered a three-bedroom flat on the gigantic Woodberry Down Estate, claimed to be one of the largest in the world. Up the Seven Sisters Road, block after block stood there, like some massive prison – all dead, treeless and with long balconies stretching along the blocks, but none to sit on so you really felt trapped unless you just stood and leaned out from the communal balcony. But hey, it was a home and the first real one after almost three years of living in rooms, attics and relatives' spare bedrooms. Now we had a place of our own and we were deliriously happy. It was exciting to move into a new area and a completely different life. We were nicely positioned on the fourth floor and for us it was a paradise.

At last I had a room of my own after many years of sharing or squatting on my put-u-up. I was determined to make my room as personal and unique as possible so the very next morning I took a bus to Stamford Hill, N16, which was to be the manor of my social conditioning for the next seven years. There, I checked all the furniture shops for a table lamp to place next to my bed so I could read.

The flats were not yet centrally heated so coal was delivered once a week. We had a fire in the living room that invariably belched out smoke the wrong way as if suffering from indigestion until it was properly burning while the rest of the flat froze. Mum would sit right on top of it, legs apart and roasting herself – which unfortunately had the effect of making me feel slightly queasy.

To get into our flat at Keynsham House you took the lift to the fourth floor and then walked along the balcony past the front doors of all the neighbours until you came to ours. But there were no gardens, so in summer all you could do to get a breath of fresh air was step outside the front door. But I loved my room and did my best to decorate it and make it into a congenial kids' den. The kitchen was small, but we had a fridge for the first time in our lives, which was most exciting. Eventually we even had a phone, but we had to share it with the next-door neighbours since in those days they didn't have enough numbers to go around and it was called a 'party-line'. Naturally this caused a few problems and eventually after much pleading, we got our own phone: Stamford Hill 6860, our very first phone!

Now, for the first time in three years, the family was reunited. Each morning I would go to school: Hackney Downs Grammar was a fair old schlepp, which necessitated getting the 653 bus to Hackney and then a long solemn walk to the back end of the school. There, we would all gather in the playground until the bell went and we filed into our classrooms.

Since this was a huge housing scheme for the East End, naturally quite a few of the tribe were living around us; I even had a school friend (Brian Press) living in the same block. It was a simple life, yet in many ways a nourishing one. Dad bought a black-and-white TV, which was one of the most exciting things to happen to us yet and radically changed our lifestyles and habits; we fastened ourselves to it nearly every night. There was just one channel, the BBC, and it only came on after 6pm but what we saw was invariably interesting. At least twice a week a drama kept us all totally involved and in those days you could hear every word the actors spoke. The area was well catered for in terms of cinemas, boys' clubs and dancehalls and though the standards were basic, we wanted for nothing.

We did have a bath but we had to heat the water in a boiler first to get hot water, which would then be transferred via huge pots to the bath. Dad had returned to the fold and once again I had to get used to having this belligerent man in the house. Beryl was now a 19-year-old who was always at the kitchen sink, her ample tits hanging out (which at my age I could not appreciate too much), but the poor thing had to bathe and the bath wasn't always available. However, she was quick to find a job since she was a very good typist, speedy at shorthand and apparently a first-class secretary. I do believe she could have gone on to university since she had such a gift for language: her letters from America had kept Ma and me quite enthralled and we would read them over and over again. But Dad's mantra was 'work' and maybe a great opportunity was lost: poor Beryl was swallowed up into the world of dull offices until such time as she would get married – my parents' limited vision really didn't go much beyond that.

Dad's fortunes had changed somewhat since he and his friend Morrie Bodinetz, with whom we once stayed in Luton, opened up a small menswear shop in Leman Street, just by Aldgate. It was called, rather elegantly, Bodinetz and Berks Tailors. I was so very proud of this new change in our fortunes that I took the 653 all the way to Aldgate just to look at it. Dad, of course, seemed to have no interest in taking us down to see it. I noticed the sign had misspelled menswear (ware) and so I eagerly rushed home and couldn't wait to tell him – I think for a couple of moments I was in his grace and the painter subsequently changed it.

What is a suit but a kind of outer skin, a coat or a bird's plumage as it matures and seeks to attract suitable females to its exotic and glorious image. The outer suggests inner strength, virility and robust health. So I suppose a young man going into puberty and desperately wishing to be attractive to the female race seeks any and every way to enhance his outer image. In other words, I was simply *dying* for a suit: I had to have a suit, I was gasping for a suit, a proper grown-up elegant suit similar to those I saw on the backs of all my 'pals' while I was still strutting around in bum-freezers and old grey school pants.

So, with regularity I begged, '*Please*, Dad, just any suit, Dad!' But I was still at school, with no money to go out and buy anything and was at the very vulnerable age when a young man's needs are so desperate, so great, so much the beginning and the end of the world. One is helpless and must rely on the kindness of others. So once again I became a beggar to Dad, who now had a nice little menswear shop and without too much effort could have got a local tailor to knock one up for me; and how grateful I would be, how very grateful. For whatever reason this need became the sole focus of my life: the suit would define me, in some way it would be my rite of passage, it would show the world that I had become a man! And so it gnawed at me, all the more so when I saw my local brethren at Stamford Hill neatly and beautifully dressed in blue gabardine and barathea while I still walked about in my old brown suit from childhood.

'Oh *please*, Dad!' I begged and whined and cajoled. But it was always, 'Yes, *soon*, very soon! Leave me alone right now, but soon, yes, OK, soon…' And this was the mantra I heard over and over again. However, one day he actually said: 'Come down to the shop and you can try on a suit' –once again a customer had not picked one up – 'Come down and try it on, and if it fits then I'll think about it.' Oh, with what joy and anticipation I flew down there on Saturday, being at school the rest of the week. I entered the shop and he looked at me as if I was some kind of curse but gave me the suit to try on.

Now what he didn't explain was that the suit had been made for a Caribbean and was in fact a ZOOT SUIT! This means it was a lovely royal blue gabardine but it had a fingertip jacket and the pants were very wide at the knees and very narrow at the bottom since this was the style then for the black immigrants. I came out of the fitting room in sheer delight even though I felt it was indeed just a little strange to see a fourteen-year-old boy in a zoot suit!

Dad glanced at me and realised how absurd I looked, even just a little grotesque, although it fitted me. And just because it was a suit, I didn't give a damn in hell how it looked; it was a lovely colour, it would be fine. But Dad insisted, 'No, it's not right for you; it's *definitely* not at all right for you! Take it off and I'll make you one.' But no, I just couldn't believe him any more and my passion to have something on my back there and then overcame any other consideration. I wanted it, I begged for it and said it was fine – I didn't want to wait any more. Meanwhile, the lovely and benign Morrie Bodinetz, his partner, was in the shop while all this was going on. Finally, Dad gave in to my desire. 'Fuck off, then!' he told me. Morrie looked hurt for me and I never forgot that look, but I was used to Dad and it didn't so much as touch me since I now had my suit, my beloved zoot suit.

Poor Dad, he just couldn't help it and the shop at that time wasn't taking too many orders and what with the money that was leaking out to the bookmaker's, which was all too temptingly on the first floor, he was in a sour mood. He probably looked at me and really, what he might have seen was his own shame. I am sure he would eventually have made one for me but at that time I had no more of that rare quality called patience. So what he saw may have made him ashamed to let his son go out onto the street looking halfway between a joke and a pimp when his own father was a tailor. But he did give me a suit and for that, I was grateful.

Eventually Dad agreed to make me a suit of my own, provided I paid for the cost. So I had to save every penny, which took well over a year and was only achieved by staying in every single night – shades of the story of the bicycle and 40 days' good behaviour! In the end he did make me a navy suit, which wasn't too bad.

Grocers Company Grammar School, Hackney Downs

I was, in fact rather glad to leave Raines Foundation School since I was starting to acquire ink entries again and preferred to get out than put up with that stupid adult violence against me. It was a bit of a journey to Hackney Downs where my new school, an old, imposing Victorian building, was situated. I met the headmaster, Mr Baulk – a highly respected man whom I found tetchy and self-important, with what would turn out to be an exceedingly mean streak in him. The next great shock of my life was when for no good reason I was relegated to the 'C' group although I had been in the 'A' group of a far superior establishment. Why could they not have given me an exam to show some kind of standard? But no, straight into the 'C' group it was, with a very strange bunch of kids, some of whom were misfits and one daft bastard who wanted to fight with me almost as soon as I got there.

On my first day I sat there in complete and utter misery and disbelief, so much so that I actually felt defiled. I recall crossing that miserable patch of land called Hackney Downs at lunchtime and getting the bus home, weeping most of the way. Ma said not to worry, this was only a way of testing me and no doubt next term they would obviously relegate me to my correct station in life. But it was not to be: I was left to rot, neglected and treated as a third-class citizen by the teachers. From that day on, I lost all desire to learn, my pride diminished and the canker set in; I hated that school with a vengeance and just put up with it. I could not make friends with any in the class except perhaps one boy, who was a little friendly but had his allegiance elsewhere. Weekends were one pure hell of loneliness.

⫯

Stamford Hill
For centuries Jewish families have lived in Stamford Hill but this accelerated in the 1880s when the Jews en masse began to leave the End End and its poverty behind and arrive and settle there.

It was a more desirable option, given its relative prosperity and the attractive dwellings, following a period of development that began in 1800.

Stamford Hill continued to welcome Jews of different denominations and has since become the centre of the Ashkenazi orthodox Jewish community, which is today in the region of 20,000-strong. Amazingly, it also contains the largest Hasidic community in Europe. The community of Stamford Hill is very mixed and has opened its doors to every people, who seem to live alongside each other with relatively little friction, no mean feat.

—◆—

Just a mile or so from Manor House, Stamford Hill was to be my main source of social activity for the next nine years and thus the 'Hill' shaped me largely, fed my curiosity, developed my relationships with friends, both male and female and encouraged me to be a bit bolder. As well as corrupting me, it shaped my values, gave me many days (and nights) of joy, larks, games, jousts. In short, it was a small but perfect society, sharing all the values and blemishes inherent in any society. It also taught me how to grow with friends, many of whom I remember with great fondness, half a century later.

Manor House was the mouldy hub of three dull areas of grey London suburbia, from Finsbury Park to the West and renowned for the magnificent Astoria cinema which felt like a wonderland. Whenever you entered the great foyer it was as if you were in a demi-paradise, with fountains and gilt cupids. Upstairs around the side were fantastic animals, cupolas and minarets, while the entire roof was fretted with stars. I had never seen anything quite like it – even before the movie started, you were already transported.

Apart from this temple to film, the rest was a decayed suburb. There was, however, the great open area of Finsbury Park, a wonderful escape where I loved to wander. To the north stretched an area of endless suburbia and identical streets called Wood Green, Palmers Green, Bounds Green (which was beginning to sprout a few more exotic shoots of Cypriot, Turkish and Greek culture) and the drab lands of Stoke Newington to the East, redeemed only by its park. So my main area of adventure was Stamford Hill, with its largely Jewish population, which seemed to be the first stop when the Jews of the East End decided to escape the narrow streets of the ghetto in search of greener pastures.

Just off Stamford Hill was a rather rundown youth club where if you were bored and had nothing better to do (which was most of the time), you could just wander in. It did little to stimulate young minds except keep them out of mischief, but at least you could sit and chat to the young girls and play billiards on the small table. However, you could also drink tea and waste an hour or two and meet other wastrels your own age. With my taste for the exotic or the outside, I made friends with a strange little chap who was a child actor and called himself Malcolm Knight, although his real name was Zauseman. He had a royal blue gabardine suit, blue suede shoes and wore his hair in a large greasy quiff – he was what you might call a bit of a character. Malcolm was about the same age as me, about 13 or 14 and spoke with a most affected accent, but he was very charming and we became firm friends.

He was the first boy I knew to carry his own printed cards! Since he was so bizarre, I found him very attractive to be with. We fooled around a lot, chatted endlessly, flirted with the young girls in the club and took lots of photos of each other doing silly things, like pretending to climb into the local bank. Few others had much time for him but since I was always attracted to eccentrics, we got along really fine. I somehow admired him for what he had already achieved but soon I was to discover another world, which was the community of Stamford Hill, which centred on the 'Hill' itself, whose meeting place was the pinball saloon, affectionately nicknamed the 'shtupp' house. *Shtipp* or *shtupp* being Yiddish for 'push', since one was always pushing the pinball machines to get a higher score, much to the annoyance of the owner Bill, who fretted for his beautiful machines and if the money changer, a long skeleton called Phil, caught you then you could be exiled for a month. Mind you, for some '*shtupp*' would have some rather more colourful sexual connotation…

So I started to hang around the shtupp house, meeting other kids, playing for pennies on the machine or trying our skills on the mini-hockey table. This is where I came across Paul Joseph, known as 'Ginger Paul' on account of his luxurious mop of red hair. As a youth he was extraordinarily handsome and everyone was attracted to him, but he was a boy with absolutely no morals, beliefs or ambition except to amuse himself and others. He even made up his own cockney language, which was the funniest thing I ever heard. This was a boy who loved himself to death and I'd often see him hanging around outside the shtupp house, doing nothing except waiting. 'Waiting for Godot', you might say, until he was joined by another, until there was a small group. He fancied himself as a bit of a tough guy whereas he was a true softy, but with his perfect profile and red hair he looked like perfect material for a young gangster.

Barry Wise became another friend. With his dark, saturnine features, he was very good-looking and quite a tough, streetwise kid. He was a source of unending admiration as I was still a novice on the battleground and hadn't yet won my spurs, so to speak. Since fear speaks louder than words on Stamford Hill, the pecking order was strictly obeyed and how I yearned to be part of it. But it wasn't too long before I was tested when a rather large guy at the club who always liked to harass and bully me provoked me enough for me to forget my fears; my response was immediate and fierce. Before long, he was on the floor, whimpering for mercy. To my astonishment I then realised that perhaps I was tougher than I thought, that all those years of training and swimming had turned me into a stalwart youth.

The young men who seemed to be those to whom everybody looked up to were the 'Guv'nors'. One was 'Moisher' – a short, bizarre-looking creature who reminded me of Popeye, with his broken flattened nose, pale blue eyes and broad round jaw. He had a very strange look, both babyish and fierce (a bit like a cross cat) and seemed to do nothing but stand around Stamford Hill and wait. Moisher was never less than immaculately turned out in the fashionable Yankee style, with slacks turned up at the cuff, white sox, shiny black shoes and usually an open-collar soft grey shirt, beneath which peeked a white T-shirt. His hair, always fluffy and clean, was the current mode of the time, with a quiff just hanging over the forehead. Invariably his prop was a rolled-up newspaper, which for some reason he kept by his side. He seemed to find just about everything amusing. Tough beyond his size, he appeared quite fearless and with his odd, raspy voice, he might have been more comfortable in Brooklyn than Stamford Hill.

Then there was Ronnie Mitchell, who was also blessed with good looks: equally tough, he possessed the mandatory walk, which was swinging from the hips to the left and to the right as if balancing himself on a ship in buoyant seas. Another was Harry Lee, who seemed definitely odd, with a streak of the demonic about him; everyone was wary of him. He seemed quite fearless, however. And so these three policed our domain while we novices would gather admiringly, if not timidly around them.

There were two cinemas on the 'Hill': the large Regent on the crossroads, where everybody seemed to go on the Monday for some reason, and the Super on the other side, everybody's choice on a Sunday afternoon and where you'd take your girlfriend, if you were lucky enough to have one. And in the summer it was the custom to cruise round Springfield Park for the occasional chat-up. Stamford Hill contained quite an exotic mixture of nations since all the Jews were still more or less second generation whose parents had recently pulled themselves out of the East End and so there were among others, second-generation Russian Jews, Spanish Jews, Polish Jews and Rumanian Jews. One or two had even become film extras, which to us was the equivalent of a movie star.

One such person was Joey Slavid, then handsome beyond belief. Whenever he came up the 'Hill' he was immaculately dressed, his hair perched high and no less than a powdered face after a close shave. I believe it must have taken him hours to get ready – he even had a movie-star voice, so elegant and charming. And all you could do was to inconspicuously follow him, which was only to the cafe round the corner, where he'd hold court and do impressions of his hero, Tony Curtis. Then he'd go back to the shtupp house and we'd all dutifully follow. His manners were as beautiful as his looks, as is frequently the case with excessively good-looking people as if being charming is a way to compensate for nature's bounty.

There was one more boy with excessively good looks, though he was small. He had the most perfect Spanish-looking features and that was Garry Gross. Sad to say, all these wickedly handsome men bloomed for only a short period before their looks were blown away with the sand. In later years Joe Slavid worked as a croupier and was still trying to get bit parts, but he remained as charming as ever.

Hebrew Classes

Naturally, Ma wished me to continue my Hebrew classes and enrolled me at the Egerton Road Synagogue, where such classes were held two to three evenings a week. I was coming up to the age of 13, when it was expected that 'decent' Jewish boys would have a Bar Mitzvah, which is a ritual signifying the arrival of manhood and is in fact vital, even in the most unorthodox of Jewish families. Those who did not, for whatever reason, were perceived to be 'out of the fold' or beyond the pale, even non-men. The ritual was a mark or arrival: you would need to study to read a small portion of the Torah and make a speech, that is all.

It has become a little too much an act of triumphalism in many Jewish families, whose fathers would rather spend a fortune on the ceremony and invite scores of friends and distant relations than keep it quiet and respectful for the sake of the son. Now it is all about the 'growing' of the dad. However, in my case after several months of study, a Bar Mitzvah was never mentioned and obviously without at least some encouragement or someone to explain what I had to do, the time just drifted away. Now I seldom attended the classes and my thirteenth birthday arrived with that precious day as fruitless and pointless as any other. A small home ceremony would have sufficed but Dad, probably believing the cost would be enormous, shunned it. And so I was never Bar Mitzvah'd, never made a 'man'. The shame of it has stayed with me till this day.

Mercifully, school was coming to an end and I had little to show for it except three long wasted years spent among the inmates. I believe the teacher couldn't help but categorise the 'C' group as morons and swiftly disabuse us of any hopes we might cherish for ourselves, any frail ambitions. Even Joe Brierly, who was famously Harold Pinter's teacher and even guru, saw fit to give us morons only grammar and seldom, if ever, creative writing or the stories that so lit up my mind when divine Miss Parry read to us in Christian Street School – just mechanical grammar so we would be of use in non-creative jobs in offices. However, one day he did give us an essay to write and so I did, though somewhat half-heartedly. When he read it, he looked me in the eye and actually said: 'I've wasted all these years when I should have encouraged you to write.' Ha, ha – too late, mate! Encouraged by his attitude at least, I asked him to write a reference for me so that I might get a job. 'Write me a poem', he said, 'and I'll do one for you'. The weeks went by and my creative spirit had long withered, but I thought I'd better deliver so I actually copied something out of a book of poems. Of course the clever old dog sniffed it out right away.

Then it was over, school was finished: no farewells, no cele-brations, nothing. No handshakes, no pats on the back, no 'keep in touch', no reunions – a big empty nothing. I had learned little since Raines Foundation in Stepney: my gift for language squandered, having been taught by a bullying lunatic called 'Dodo'. His name was actually De La Feld. In fact, I had retrogressed into a delinquent demi-criminal class. A spotty-faced slob, I had no ambition nor had any ambition been stoked in me and I was to face the next five years of my life without it. It would be a desert, a wilderness but then, only then it would change since I believed I still had one small spark left inside of me that would not go out. It kept me ever so slightly awake, but only just. But now I had to get a job, now I would face the horrors of such ill preparation from school and sadly, even from Dad. I was fit for nothing. So I bought the *Evening Standard* and looked up the vacancies: 'Desk clerk wanted…'

Shirley
The one really positive thing that kept a small flame alive in my head, something worthwhile, had been Shirley. It was

taken for granted: we truly loved each other and she was mine just as I was hers; I expected her letters as she expected mine, it was as simple as that. In fact we cared for each other so much that I had no doubt one day we would marry. However, there is no accounting for the well-meaning interference of others, even those closest to you, to really fuck it up, to undo that special if not precious bond and then hurl you into limbo. Loved ones somehow keep you in balance: they are your ballast and sometimes your anchor, they prevent you from wobbling just as the moon apparently stabilises the earth. You hold each other steady.

And thus I recall and can never forget my beloved sister coming into my room one evening. She needed to talk to me and thus she began. Not dramatically, but in a kindly, older-sister way, the sum of which was it would be better to stop this correspondence, that it was getting too serious – you are both too young and have much to do and learn, therefore it's not good for you or her. And that her letters were getting a little too 'warm' or 'intimate' (I forget which, but something implying the dreaded sex) and there would still be time later when you're older and wiser, etc., etc. And while you're still at school you must give your full mind to your studies. But the upshot of this was that I felt exposed, uncovered, like the blankets had been pulled away to reveal my nakedness, like I was some kind of dirty beast. For the first time in my life I felt shame, shame for something that was the most precious thing in my life. Shame. Thank you, Beryl!

My sister had read Shirley's letters to me, maybe shown them to Ma. Between them both they had decided this would be the best thing to do. I don't believe Ma would ever do this – in fact, she loved this relationship and the letters flitting backwards and forwards – but maybe the two women, embittered in their own quest for love, the elusive elixir that always evaded them, found it too threatening. I couldn't have been more than 13 and this is the time when guilt's arrows make their entry into soft, vulnerable places.

I had no idea what my sister was talking about since I felt no angst, stress or confusion; least of all, shame. It was she who put these feelings inside me, maybe out of some sense of responsibility, perhaps at the behest of Mum – who knows? Maybe the messenger gets all the blame and maybe it came from the girl's own parents. In the foul society of Hackney and Stamford Hill, where we were united by the pinball machine, in that wretched and drab school where I had learnt nothing and the only thing I did achieve was making a small book unit in the carpentry workshop, that was it, that's the lot. And so this correspondence with my beloved Shirley was the most nourishing, positive, loving element of my wretched life.

I felt as if I had been caught *in flagrante delicto*, a beast with a horn, and I didn't have the guts to argue or resist and continue to write; I just stopped, stopped stone dead. I was ashamed and the effect was to knock my values into a cocked hat. I have little doubt my behaviour deteriorated, became looser after that well-meaning piece of advice. From then on I believe sex was implanted in my brain as something furtive and dirty, that's what I was, and this has shaped me.

The paradox was that while the natural urge in me to love had been besmirched, there was no thought to instruct me in its brutal mechanics. In fact, I instructed myself and when one day Ma's keen eye saw the outline of a contraceptive in my wallet, I was further exposed and so all this led me down the slippery path of casual sex, the horrors of unwanted pregnancy and the pain that arose from that at the age of 15, hardly a good start in life. But curiously, I was falling in love with pretty girls even after a few passionate hugs, becoming lovesick at the drop of a hat as if something in me was broken and I was constantly trying to mend it, so even now I beg you, my darling Shirley, to forgive me.

PS: How we recall events so differently! While writing this rather intense and otiose declaration of young love I decided to ring the lady in question, who is still in Luton (I managed to find her number from the same old friend I stayed with, years ago). Thus, 60 years later, I did reach the lady on the phone and she couldn't remember anything about 'letters' and could only just remember me. Ha! Ha! Ha!

Part II

Teenage Years

So this is how it used to be! At 15, on a bench over the park: hand slowly creeping up the knee, then up the thigh, then a torturous stroll to those nether regions. Real slow, terrifyingly slow, murderously slow… Tongue meanwhile making symbolic movements in her mouth: very juicy and tasty, right arm cradling her shoulder. Will it happen? And still slow… She might push my arm away but without too much conviction, just a gesture. Oh, modesty! It was always autumn and gradually growing dark and the little park was where you went since this was your place for fumbling and groping and slithering, sliding and gushing. You had nowhere else, so you went there. Just for a stroll and a wander and passionate embraces and hot, strong kisses. Oh, those kisses, sweet as honeydew melons! And it was autumn, so it grew dark sooner, with that pungent smell of summer's end, which was damp rotting leaves, the pond in the centre of the park and maybe a cigarette – a Players, or a Churchill or a Gold Flake, each had their own peculiar flavour – and of course the exotic smell of her make-up, her cheap cologne, her hair and the lipstick. All that was the smell of sex, that hoary, pungent, sickly-sweet smell of sex. And now my fingers are slowly unravelling the various layers like so many skins before, reaching the forbidden fruit. Oh, how sweet and gurgly it feels… Oh, how dreamy, how awesomely wonderful in a teenager's imagination are the lubric, intimate parts of the female.

And my tongue now deeper in her mouth and her tongue goes in mine so we do a part exchange. My imagination is now aflame, for never have I touched a female intimately before. Oh God, wonderful! The moon is lying on its side in the middle of the pond and now a wind is sneaking round my ears, the streetlights from the main road are being beaten up in the water, along with the moon. Somebody walks by: my hand stops and she pulls her coat over my anatomical investigations; the steps recede, my hand continues. She feels truly wonderful – marvellous, silky, lovely, delicate. And she's really sweet and I'm lucky tonight: I've pulled, like I won a prize! And I'm glowing and rampantly randy to score. I'm so lucky! I've scored a delicious female. Usually it's just a kiss and the occasional tit squeeze and if you're lucky you can cuddle against a wall or a tree. That can be real good 'cos you can thrust yourself against her strong young body and feel her mound of Venus and that is really exciting and if she likes you she will allow you to exercise your passion, to grind against her until your brain explodes in a shower of stars. Over the skirt of course, but then you have her in your hands and if she likes you… You couldn't slide a leaf between you: like two powerful magnets, you are drawn to each other like a vice and strangely it feels as if there's nothing between you as you grind and squeeze her cheeks and ram your tongue as deep as you can down her throat. And she wiggles her tongue inside yours and it's heaven since there's nothing in the world like this. Is there anything better to life than this? This is why I live; this is the consummation of my night.

I stood on Stamford Hill and made small, lifeless, stupid-idiot chatter and played the slot machines, watching the steel balls bounce from one electric reel to another and listening to the jukebox forever playing the same wretched song. In the summer it was practically played all day and it was Frankie Lane singing 'Jezebel'. And all the girls on Stamford Hill were like versions of Jezebel, sickly-sweet smelling, possessing those unguent dark places that teenage boys toss their cabers over. But then she chatted and we had a coffee, maybe in the café round the corner and chatted more and listened to Frankie Lane, or Guy Mitchell or Johnny Ray.

Then it's 'Fancy a walk?' 'Ooh er… OK, just for a little while…' Or it was behind the council flats in Manor House in the dark, kissing goodnight and her aware of my lust and aware of her own lust, knowing how important it was for the boy to consummate his and then be calm and quiet.

Hugging her against a hard object until there's only the two of us in the world and there's only our two fires in the world and nothing else exists nor matters except the lava churning inside both of us. And you lean against her as if she is your milk and sustenance, your life and oxygen, your meaning and reason. It feels like you're fucking the life out of her – except you're not fucking her at all, you're squeezing and rubbing and soaring and almost crying until that moment, yes and at that moment nothing in the whole darned world is of more vital importance to you.

Nothing more fantastic, more thrilling than that moment and yes, suddenly she feels like paradise, you have a piece of heaven in your arms. It's a revelation… Now in the park, on the bench in late autumn on a chilled foggy night, it's less frenzied since my hands flutter over her body like a butterfly fluttering from flower to flower. But I'm not yet so experienced, not yet… It took some time before she yearned for me, before she could bring herself to explore those unfamiliar parts of a rampant young man. But for now my imagination does it for me: it touches me, it ignites me; it illuminates me. And we kissed and squeezed each other like nothing else existed in the whole world but the two of us.

It had been a nice night, one of those drifty weeknights when it was still a little warm early in the evening and you just had jackets on and the girls a funny waist-length coat. Since I had nothing else to do, nowhere else to go, nothing to occupy my mind, nothing to study, to play, to paint, to create, nothing that would draw the curiosity out of me, nothing to pull the wonderment out of me, nothing that would or might identify me as an artist – a pianist, a dancer, a carpenter, a singer – nothing to take an interest in, I thought I'd jump on the 653 and head down to Stamford Hill. Maybe and even probably, I would find another wastrel, another useless, mindless slob like myself looking for company and *hang out* together outside the amusement arcade where we would *hang out,* chat and play the pin tables; that's where we'd go, especially on weeknights. Not much else to do really, so you'd go to the arcade and kind of *hang about* and *hang about* and look and wait and *hang about…* Sure enough, some mates would come by and so you'd all waste life and *hang about* together and play some pinball and that could be fun, especially if you're playing for a penny a point! Then you could make a few bob, that's if you were good – and I was pretty damned good. That is not to say our lives were totally useless since once or even twice a week we'd go jiving and that needed skill and some attitude and careful movement with the girls, who like a good jiver. So here I am just talking about a night where we didn't see a film or go jiving, or stay in and watch telly.

In other words, just a night where you simply breathed, jumped on a bus, walked, played the pinball machine or even a disk on the jukebox. And if blonde Nita was there, you could even have a small dance in the corner until 'Bill' the owner would stop you. But if you misbehaved or 'tilted' his precious pinball machines once too often or generally pissed about, he might 'ban' you for a month and then you'd have to stand outside like a chump, like a nomad.

So for a while you were in purgatory and hung about outside his cancerous arcade like a leper. Who cares? He's been pushing up daisies for a long time now. They're all pushing up daisies now, aren't they? After school I'd take the bus from my council estate and get off right outside the arcade, the shtupp house. I'd peep in first of all and usually it would only be Phil wandering around the empty arcade like a great thin shark.

There I'd hang around since this was all I knew, but I also knew when I became an adult it would come together somehow – that's what I thought, anyway. I mean I was always an optimist. Then some mates would come up whose lives were about as futile as mine, maybe even more so, not great mates but just guys you could hang with and maybe go for walks with a first-class bird or exchange useless chatter and be curious about the world going by. That was a nice thing to do and better than hanging around. So they'd come up and if it was one of my 'mates', we'd chat, decide what we'd like to do and then go to the 'A and B' café round the corner, order tea and sit on stools facing the mirror. We'd stare at ourselves, check our barnets and chat about other mates, like who had 'scored' and who was in the latest punch-up, what this one did and that one did. And then some others might pop in and then we'd go back to the arcade, which by that time might have changed its social status.

Being low down on the pecking order our attention was always on those above us: the hard men, the 'Tuff' guys, who hardly ever gave us a glance let alone the time of day. But we looked up to them, admired and feared them, wished to emulate them and even more hoped to be taken into their magic circle: the elite triumvirate of Moisher, Ronnie and Harry. All three might justly earn the epithet '*Shtarkers*' (Yiddish for 'Tuff' guys), naturally after the German for strength, being '*stark*'.

On the other hand, there was the Stamford Hill Jewish Boys' Club down the road and so just to have something to do, we'd take a walk and check it out. It was a bit of a dump in a ramshackle house but on the plus side there were always girls and if you queued, it would be possible to have a game of billiards on the one table available. So it wasn't so bad and in fact when I had my first initiation into street fighting with that long loutish slob (who has probably turned into a charming, responsible father), he was astounded by my ferocity and of course whined and reported me to the governor of the club, a rather large oaf called, as I remember, Mr 'Bunce'. Nothing came of it other than a reprimand but suddenly among the few simple oafs I hung out with I was a bit of a 'hero', even to myself. Now I was determined to test myself against some bigger game: 'I found myself to be a right proper fella', I had stepped on the first rung.

On Sunday night there was dancing in the basement to a record player but I really could not dance and hadn't yet mastered jiving, so I was a bit of a leper there too. Just watching the pretty girls and occasionally catching their eye but being unable to dance meant I had no real means of communication. This was, I could see, a rite of passage that I had to master and master it I would. Nothing on heaven and earth would hinder me from this goal and so it came to pass that one day someone introduced me to Grey's Dance Hall in Finsbury Park, where a young chap called Leslie actually taught the main jive steps to a record player and I saw it was no great mystery but a basic knowledge of three simple steps that one had to learn. Once I learnt it, I couldn't stop. Jiving became my life and of course it was your ticket to the female sex. Jiving just somehow defined you, revealed who you were, how elegant, graceful, even witty. Girls could not resist a good jiver.

But the Stamford Hill Club was OK, even if the types there were 'Softies' and a bit normal, not like the 'Tuffs' who hung around the arcade. So you'd chat and have some tea, walk about, play billiards and then walk back to the arcade since this was the pivotal point, the centre of gravity; the vortex around which we all spun like flotsam and jetsam. By then it was getting dark and little knots were gathered, laughing and fooling around, giggling at nothing. And the jukebox was playing, the pinball machines clacking and the girls were shrieking and opening up those vanity boxes they used to carry around instead of handbags. It was the rage and everybody had these big boxes for all the junk women felt it necessary to put in them. The jukebox cost two pence a go and Bill, who stood guard over his fetid empire, made sure the top tunes were in. The girls would twitch and bob to the music, just bob their heads like ducks, purse their lips and coo over Perry Como or Guy Mitchell: 'Hey round the corner – Hoo Hoo!'

The hit songs were played over and over again, driving everyone mad. Of course the most overplayed one was 'Jezebel' sung by Frankie Lane: *Jez…a…beeeell, it was you.* We could all sing the words by now. Naturally I had my own faves – in fact, lots of them – but I went a bundle on Johnny Ray and felt really connected with him as if he had tapped something deep within me, something that needed to be identified, acknowledged, that we were not alone: *If your sweetheart sends a letter of goodbyyyeeeiie, it's no secret if you sit right down and cryeeeeeiii…* I did that, oh yes and more than once since I was such a slosh bag; cried when a girl got fed up and pissed off, really heaved – had to control that, maybe I was too pussy-addicted. I was a pussy freak: I dreamed of pussy, night and day; I fantasised about girls, night and day, even at school. So that night I made some serious chat-up with one of the girls I had seen earlier at the club, so I had something to chat about, like '*Wadja do?*'

'*Secretary…*'

'*Oh yeah, that's nice and wherejalive?*'

'*Stoke Newington…*'

'*Ja like Johnny Ray?*'

'*Nah, I prefer Perry Como.*'

'*Fancy a walk?*'

'*OK, but not for long or my dad will be out looking for me.*'

'*OK, sure.*'

So we'd stroll to the small park just off the main road, and it was quiet and the pond glistened in the middle, where an occasional duck would squawk. Before long I was kissing her like my life depended on it, as if I was sucking the very life out of her lungs and she was responding like she'd been in a convent for 50 years and had just come out. Our groins were hot, mad and feverish. Within 20 seconds we loved each other. We were mad for each other, but I didn't have enough experience to understand what to do with girls yet.

I tended to rush when I should have just connected, gone for walks, to the movies, met Mum and Dad, gone dancing. That would come later, when I did in fact find a regular tart, a more-than-willing recipient of my frequent pollinations, who didn't love (or even care for me) that much.

But now as an inveterate explorer I was discovering those mysterious areas, valleys, streams and rainforests on the female continent. That was superb, I was King for the Night. Oh, tremendous! I could barely believe I had possession of this cute sweet meringue, my tongue in her lovely mouth, saliva running down my cheek. Her hand now making tentative explorations on my continent, brilliant! It was the epitome of living, the perfect end to the day. And now, at that moment, at that wonderful delirious moment in time…

'I have to go now,' she says.

'Oh, no… No, no, not just yet, darling, please…'

'No, sorry, I have to go back… I have to… Another time.'

And already she's deporting my handful of explorers, sending them out into the cold air, where their only sanctuaries are the deep pockets of young boys: your own, that is.

But there was a young woman (Roselyn) who was legendary as a conductor of the male orchestra, her skill with the 'baton' bore no comparison. She would elicit the sweetest sounds – in fact, she was proud of her reputation for squeezing the finest arias from her male members. One fine evening I asked if she might be kind enough to impart her genius to me and yes, her skills were true as the legend. Her secret lay in her innate understanding of the 'score' before her and her steady, unhurried rhythm. Naturally as a most ardent and willing pupil, I put myself entirely in her wondrous hands. I felt the closest I had ever felt to what I imagine paradise to be: this was the very first time a girl had touched me so deeply, it was unimaginably wonderful. But then a thought occurred to me that this was such an intense brilliant experience, so very moving – how on earth could those slobs up at Stamford Hill make such crude, stupid, vile comments about something so awesome? It was really spectacular and I have never forgotten that first lesson… Never, Roselyn – God bless you, girl!

Yes, it was difficult being young: such a web of pain came with the onrush of all the gifts, the discoveries, the treasures, the painful desires that hung from your neck like stones of guilt, your confusion between being a sexually rampant boy and being made to feel the most loathsome guilt in the prison that was one's home. My home, the little bedroom in a flat on the top floor, with a communal balcony stretching from one end of the building to another, but it was home for many years. The small ten-inch TV that Dad brought home one day and upon which we fastened night after night, unto which we glued ourselves. In those days I ate like an Olympic athlete in training; my appetite was voracious. Returning from school, I'd devour six beigels before supper while watching the magic black box. Those were the days of the spots, those horrific emblems of hormonal change, no doubt enriched by Ma's unwholesome greasy food. Fried salami with chips was one of her faves for me, though she did sometimes make the most delicious coleslaw, which I would devour by the bucket.

And the chicken soup was pretty good, made even better when she added the dumplings that were divine. Then there were the sandwiches for school lunch, which I ate in the large amphitheatre while playing shove-halfpenny, pronounced strangely enough 'haypnee'. The afternoon slid by, usually painlessly and fruitlessly enough except for days when we had maths or physics, which for some reason did not impede on my brains for a millisecond. Had they perhaps been presented in a way that made them the fascinating subjects they are, they might have knocked a few doors open in my skull, but the way they were taught by a bunch of elderly, sour and frustrated bastards even poisoned the subjects I might have been interested in.

I used to love French when I attended the Raines Foundation Grammar School in the East End, learned the verbs speedily and relished my absorption of another language, but the doddering, old sadistic slob in Hackney ruined my potential and that went downhill like everything else. Hackney Downs School had taken a bright imaginative child and in a couple of years turned him into a sleaze-bag yobbo.

Not having a caring or loving Dad didn't help too much either since his greatest pleasure seemed to be in continually finding fault with me. He acted as if he was some kind of indifferent stepfather and I was just a useless burden that he happened to be stuck with. Since he had opened the small East-End tailor's, he was always working and he never ceased to moan about how hard he worked to keep a parasite like me. His acid tongue scooped out lashings of bitterness and frustration, then spat them out whenever the mood got him: *'You're good for nothing – I've kept you all my life and much good it's been!'* When I actually had the temerity to respond by saying, *'I'll be keeping you one day'*, his immediate retort was: *'I'd rather die than take anything from you!'* This line I have never forgotten, not in all the years that have washed so many memories away, good and bad, savoury and unsavoury; this line etched itself too deeply into my brain. What ghosts still lurk around those filthy words or demons that come to haunt you, along with the usual like 'useless bum' and 'no good'. I could never quite understand what I had done to inspire such a wealth of vitriol but it must have been something really shocking, bad, disgusting, or at least it felt that way.

I must be rotten, vile, evil, dirty to have earned such a wealth of epithets and yes, he did work hard but the profits of his work he just spewed away at the dog track or at the card tables, at the race track or *Speilers*, those little gambling clubs where old European Jews loved to socialise and enjoy a game of bridge.

Dad was apparently a brilliant bridge player and he knew his maths. He was also brilliant at school but his own tyrant Dad had pulled him out at 14 to get him into the sweatshops, tailoring. No doubt he was cut out for much higher things. In rosier times he would do my maths homework for me – he was so clever that he could work it out in his head, but I never got the tick of approval since the teachers couldn't fathom out how I had come up with the answers.

As I grew older, I became a whipping boy for his frustration, something my sister seemed to avoid. Sometimes I even tensed up as I heard him coming through the door and was pleased not to see him when on Wednesday and Saturday nights he wouldn't come home since those were his 'Turkish bath nights' when he slept overnight, or so he claimed, at the Russell Square Turkish baths – an amazingly beautiful bath house, where you could lie on cots and be served tea and hot buttered toast after your sojourn in the steam rooms. I went there myself in later years.

Of course my poor Ma suspected he had a tart somewhere but by this time she was too weary to complain and in fact probably couldn't care less and just put up with it; simply tolerated it for the sake of peace and put her heart and soul into me, her hopes, her joy. His shouting was horrible, though I suspect he was a physical coward. In later years, when I had my own pad, I would regularly visit Ma on Sunday mornings, every Sunday morning without fail and feast on the treats she put out for me. How she loved me coming over and preparing the wonderful breakfast! I would sit in her little kitchen just off the dining room and begin with toasted buttery beigels smothered in cream cheese and smoked salmon, pickled cucumbers and olives. And then she'd serve the chicken soup… and on it would go till I bounced home like a stuffed rubber ball.

Then I might just catch the old man as he came in with his guilt offering of bags of fruit from the market. He always did that, but sadly by then I didn't have too much to say to him so we would just exchange small talk and then I'd leave. Although sometimes when he felt like it, he could switch on the charm and for some reason I still had an admiration for him, for his mathematical skills. He had moved his tiny tailor's shop to Brixton in south London – a shrewd move since he now made suits for the Caribbean community (or '*shwartzers*' as they were dismissively called by the old Jews, though this in no way was meant as a racist slur). If he'd had a good day and taken a dozen orders he would come home pleased as punch – on Sunday, of course. He would take out a fat bundle from his hip pocket. I've never seen so much money in my life. I was deeply impressed but he rarely, if ever, peeled off a note for me or maybe once. But he'd bung Ma some cash since he made sure she was never short and she would carefully stash as much as she could away.

But Dad was clever, he was OK: he could make a suit and I could make nothing, not a suit, not anything. He had absolutely no interest in teaching me tailoring and I would have been a good tailor, I'm sure, since I loved doing anything even vaguely creative and I loved fashion, even if I had hardly a jacket on my back. But it was not to be: 'You don't want to go into tailoring, a terrible business.' I seemed to hear this mantra for years, but I thought tailors have been here since the beginning of civilisation and I would have been a high-class fashion mogul, I would have a skill for something, but nothing. I had a skill for nothing, zilch. I liked art and had an aptitude but needed to be taught. 'Please, please, teach me something, just anything', but nothing, fuck all! Yeah.

Something will happen, of course it will: you'll find a way. You'll find the path one day and it will take you to the Promised Land; you'll be rich and famous one day, of course. You will… Famous and maybe even a little mad, but that goes with the territory. Don't know how just yet, but will endeavour to find out; I'll discover it, maybe by chance, buying and selling maybe, the good old Jewish way, the old way. My friend Barry Wise did just that. He was bold and rather brave; also 'Tuff' and handsome and I admired him for having all the qualities that I lacked. Guts, bravery, stamina, balls, nerve and dark hair and strong, white teeth like a Spaniard.

So Barry went down the Houndsditch Warehouse, where they sold cheap jewellery to the trade. With the pearls in a suitcase, he would go out and flog them in street markets across the river. I will always remember his patter: 'Genu-ine three-string diamanté pearls', plus all the persuasive adjectives to go with it. He had the gift and he paid me to watch and keep an eye out for the law. For this humble job he gave me a pound a day, which was pretty good then. I watched and admired the way he just got up and began shouting the merits of his wares. How did he learn to do that? Somebody must have shown him, they must have done. He was 'the Guv'nor' – what a pal to have, what *chutzpah* (cheek) – and I was not only watching but necessary, for he needed me on alert. Handsome, if troubled Barry, he never knew what he wanted out of life. He suffered inexplicable phases of depression and yet with his looks and charisma he could easily have become an actor, like those tough, charismatic New York actors from the working-class but not in London. Here, it was still too spineless, too middle-class. Those working-class heroes had not yet arrived.

Eventually, Barry became a taxi driver, just like his dad. What a waste of talent! I liked him a lot and wanted to be his good mate, even his best friend but he had another close mate. But we would seek each other out. His dad was a decent family man as I could see when I went to visit him and he praised his taxi-driver dad for bringing the quality Sunday papers into the house. Anyway, even I was reading the *Sunday Observer*, though that may have been just a tad later. So I think of Barry from time to time. He had something deep within him that he couldn't pull out and it was poisoning him – a little like me, I guess. We all have the genie deep within us that wants to escape, wants to sing and play, to dance and leap and love, to fly and soar and make magic. If the genie can't find a way out, it will only drive us crazy, rummaging around our guts like a slug in the mud.

Ginger Paul was another. Under that thick mop of red fiery hair he had a perfect profile and with his blue eyes and long lashes, he was just so utterly handsome. He really was a friend but he had a strange ambition to be a something of a tearaway, which the poor boy never was, not even for an instant. Yet he harboured this desire to be one of the gang, to hang out with the heavy mob at The Lyceum and get in with 'Curly King' who definitely was the Guv'nor. A short, muscly young man with masses of curly hair piled up on his head like a mushroom cloud and small piercingly dark eyes. To me he was like the devil incarnate. But no matter since Paul was such a brilliant comic: with his ability to make up whole sentences and with his make-believe language as audacious as it was expressive, he became a kind of court jester to those of less-ready wit. I laughed till the tears came running down my face. He lived with his family in some decent flats, just off the main zone where the arcade was and when I met his dad he behaved like he was a bit of an old tearaway himself and so he probably inspired poor Paul's fantasies.

In some ways I loved him for his cheek, his repertoire and his craziness but he never seemed to be interested in girls except maybe to dance with and maybe, although I never knew, shag the odd one. They all fell in love with him because he was just so beautiful. I remember a hot sweaty club in the West End and I was jiving and sweating my bollocks off; I looked up and he was simply immaculate, his greased hair perched on top of his forehead, not a bead of sweat in sight – just gliding away with real cool steps, looking every inch a prince. But then he upgraded himself to the 'Tuff' brigade, entered their domain and spoke less and less to me. But everybody knew Ginger Paul and when he died of leukaemia at the age of 21, we knew him even more, as his legend grew.

And then I actually had another mate: a really sweet and funny guy, a comedian to his fingertips, with an outrageously funny face called Harold. Emotionally, he was far more in tune with me than the others who might have thought of him as a bit of a nerd. But I adored Harold and we really got on. Every week we would go to the Royal Dance Hall in Tottenham. In fact, Harold introduced me to tea dancing, which they had on Saturday afternoons.

The Royal Tottenham

For 94 years, 415–419 High Road, Tottenham, London N17 was a leading entertainment venue. In 1925 it was converted into a dance hall known as the Tottenham Palais. Later it was bought by Mecca Dance and became the Tottenham Royal, north London's premier spot for big band and swing music. In the 1950s the Royal became the centre of the Teddy-Boy era, the era that I knew. For years we would hardly miss a Saturday night at the Royal until one day we discovered the charms of the West End and advanced to The Lyceum Dance Hall in The Strand.

Oh, my beloved 'Royal' dance hall in Tottenham! Could any university give as much stimulus as that great hall where the hungry spirits of youth gathered for their seasonal rites? My old friend Harold Harris introduced me to this place when I was still 14 and to enter its huge belly was to be almost overcome with the sense that somehow you had entered a demi-paradise where scores of nymphs swirl and almost float in the sable gloom.

Oh, those glorious and mostly immortal females, primped, pampered, preened and smelling of the forests, the gardens

111

or the orchards whence they came. And to think, to even imagine maybe one of these divinities might be yours, encircled in your arms at the end of the night and most of all and surmounting all imagination, that you might actually put your arm around one of those delicious fairies just for the asking of a dance.

When we entered the hallowed portal of The Royal, Tottenham, we felt as if we were embarking on an adventure, the climax of which was securing an amiable, scented, soft, luscious female as a reward for our endeavours, for all the frustrations of the week; the bitterness of our lives, the boredom, failure, the emptiness for now as our temple, our Nirvana… at last! We paid our few shillings at the door and entered and it never, not once, lacked that sense of excitement, of anticipation, the thrill since this was where you were meant to be. This was where your body served its purpose in dancing, in sliding round the great room in anti-clockwise fashion, holding your prey. And if the dance was slow, really holding on and sliding your thigh between hers and maybe, yes, just maybe if she liked you, she might let you contact her mound of Venus as your leg thrust hers before she withdrew and then, ah heaven! You could actually *feel* her, feel the centre of her being. On a rare occasion she might even thrust her pelvis back at you and how nice is that? So this is what we looked forward to, this scent of hundreds of mixed odours and soft arms and moving hips.

My maternal grandparents.

Blind Uncle Alf with his sister and wife.

Alf in the ring with Jimmy Wilde at Holborn Stadium.

My Uncle Sam Senate's gigantic mansion in New York, 1924. My mother is second from left with her sister Doris. My father is standing by the window in the foreground.

Dad at 26.

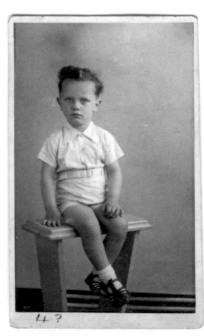

Me at four.

Mum's sister Aunty Ray.

The Senate's mansion.

DAD. THE MASTER TAILOR.

Dad grafting.

My sister Beryl and I, around 1946.

Happy days at Black Rock swimming pool, Brighton, with my sister and a friend.

East End 1948/1949 with a couple of school chums.

My Tony Curtis period.

My good mate Barry Wise.

PX days – hanging out with the workers in Bitburg, Germany.

With Mum and Dad at a formal wedding, aged 18.

As a bored steward on a cruise liner, 1956.

Fay Wasserman – sweet romance.

First acting publicity shot.

Mum, my sister and I at about 21.

But before we went in we had to adjust our quiffs since this was most important. And so we'd stand in front of the mirror and re-arrange our carefully prepared barnets that might have suffered some disarray on the journey from Stamford Hill, by bus to Tottenham. Then we'd stroll ever so nonchalantly in. Ray Ellington would be playing, introducing each number with his usual charm, especially when he announced a slow one with a cheeky, low-voiced suggestive air and then the lights would dim.

So Harold and I became mates and we would go there every Saturday night, even sometimes on a Saturday tea dance. I liked his weird sense of humour, with his clown-like face topped off with a squat nose and slightly bulging eyes. The girls found him unthreatening and cute. He nearly always had a bit of cigarette paper on his lip where it had pulled away from the fag. He'd spend hours arranging that bird's nest perched on top of his head and he had a real funny walk. Everybody did then: it was your signature. But what made Harold stand out from the others was his ability to play the alto sax, something that he was learning diligently although when I heard him practise, it made a hell of a noise and I could only assume he had the most devoted mum and dad.

The Royal, Tottenham, this souk of sweaty bodies, this seraglio of sexual temptation, also had a curious ritual whereby the dance hall was divided into two nations. On the left were the

Jews from Stamford Hill, Stoke Newington, Dalston and Hackney; on the right, the 'Gentiles' from Tottenham and distant chilly lands further north. The two regions never mixed and rarely did you go over to the other side, the enemy, unless you were a stupid dope like me. And so the place was peaceful so long as you stuck to your side of the border. I was tempted to flit over once or twice and ask for a dance but there was never any trouble since I believe nobody paid any attention to the callow youth wearing a funny suit.

The night was for us celebrating who we were: the roles we had chosen to play were allowed out since this was our stage. We were dudes, studs, young 'Tuffs', movie stars in our fantasy; gangsters, lotharios, Rudolph Valentinos, Alan Ladds, coiffed and shampooed. This was the greatest mating ritual in history. Most girls came with their mates but there would be a scattering of sad singles up at the far end near the entrance and it was wise to sniff around for some spare meat, especially when there was only half an hour left to go and you hadn't yet scored. *Oh, quick, anything, please! I need you… more than anything in the world.* 'Can I take you home?' was the usual (and only) line. If they said yes and it was within spitting distance of my council estate, great! So we'd gather outside and wait for the flaming bus since I never, ever had such a thing as wheels of my own.

And then we were there and so it began: round the back of the house for the goodnight squeeze and soon she was in my arms

114

and all was at peace, the world, the drama, the work, the traffic, the family… since the world was in my arms, my arms. I kissed her slowly at first and then more strongly and she opened her mouth and I sucked her tongue into my mouth and gently bit on it, then pressed my crotch into hers. If she didn't pull away all was wonderful since I knew she would allow me to crush, to move, to grind myself into her until the sweet time came. Didn't matter that my genie was trapped inside my trousers, didn't matter at all since it still felt wonderful and she lifted her hips slightly so she too could feel my engorged beast against her bone and let me work myself into a frenzy since she knew it would be best to let this hot, dirty little boy writhe like a snake, that's what he wants. I could smell her body through her dress, through her mouth, through her hair and I swivelled myself into her and adored her, braced myself as if I would levitate and I knew this night I would be safe.

And then it was over, over. I was back on earth. Then 'Goodnight' – how quickly it goes by, how quickly and then home and sometimes a long walk. And would I see her again? Never, never, alas… although one or two I did. And in the immortal words of Johnny Ray: *Gee, but it's great to be walking out late, walking my baby back home, arm in arm…*

At last I finished at Hackney Downs School with no fuss, no celebration (it was a month before my fifteenth birthday). What a waste of time that was, what an utter bore it turned out to be. I had started out full of joy, excitement and promise: I had passed my 11 Plus (which put me in an 'A' grade), I bought a satchel for my homework just like I used to see in the Yankee movies when some freckled snotty-nosed spoilt drip took a pile of books home. I still recall the great trip to the store (Gamage's at Gardiner's Corner, Aldgate), where Mum laid out precious pounds for my school blazer with the badge on the front and my school cap – I was pleased as punch. That was in the East End of course, at Raines Foundation and I can never forget the excitement of that first day and how surprised I was that the rest of the class for some reason didn't seem to share my enthusiasm for homework. I worked like a demon and was fascinated to be learning the mysteries of a foreign tongue, which felt so 'grown-up' and thus went mad for French, but the rest was a bit hopeless.

Each day I went to school with a will to learn: to be clever, to be a great student. However, there was always a fly in the ointment – I had never forgotten the thrashing with a cane, those awful strokes for absolutely zilch, merely talking in class just once too often. It was the worst beating I ever had. After that, things went downhill and I was only too glad to leave the school when Ma managed to get on the housing list and we moved to Manor House and a vast council estate in north London.

I was really intoxicated with the freedom of possessing my own room. Meanwhile, I had changed school and still could not get over my humiliation at being placed in 'C' grade after my success at Raines. This completely demoralised me and I felt I was with a bunch of hopeless losers and morons. 'Work well and you'll be upgraded,' I was told and although I did try at first, I had lost the will. The teachers were so unpleasant and so inept, as if they couldn't be bothered to try too hard with a 'C' group. All the curiosity I had, the passion for language and art, just faded and so I bumbled along, half-alive. I took time off, pissed about, waited for the endless summer holidays and mixed with the local morons on Stamford Hill. There could be no greater waste of a young boy's eagerness and passion, let alone talent. I would have learned more behind the bars in a zoo since that is what I felt I was: a caged beast.

At my second school more years of drift, frustration and idleness passed with little input into what I should, or could be. And then one day I was sent up to the headmaster, a Mr Baulk, for a caning for some obscure crime, the details of which I can scarce remember. However, this time I politely refused his command to bend over. Quite frankly, I had had enough of this barbaric madhouse of a school with its sadistic barmy teachers and I told him that since my father didn't beat me (a lie), neither would he. For the first time in my life I felt an enormous sense of empowerment. It was this very moment when I became a man, I am sure. No one would abuse me again, either physically or verbally. All you have to do is say no to anything or anyone who wishes to abuse or degrade you, or even violates your principles – it is a lesson I have never forgotten.

So the shocked Mr Baulk sent me home, which for me was a distinct pleasure. However, my father was sent for and it felt strange to see Dad there since it was the first time I had ever seen him have any input whatsoever in my life. So they chatted and I was reinstated and of course never caned or threatened with it ever again. But for this act of transgression the sour old sod would one day take revenge in the most puerile way, which I shall duly mention.

My time at the Grocers' School, as it was so-called, was a deeply lonely one until I made mates on Stamford Hill. But in the early days I was bitterly lonely and could barely endure the weekends that stretched out forever. At that stage, I simply had no friends and couldn't seem to make them. Whenever a new boy came into the school who had been relocated much like myself, I palled up to them, wanting them to be my friend, my special friend. I had no friends at home and my father was seldom there – and besides, he was more a hostile enemy than a friend – so I was left to my own resources. It was not particularly healthy but I endured the situation. My loneliness was a bitter fruit I had to eat and what a terrible thing that is, even for an adult with many resources at their disposal. For a child, it is remorseless. It's a terrible curse to feel unwanted, a leper. I was also bullied at one time until I got my balls in order and struck back; that was most satisfying. Then it got quiet.

Like any school, there were some nice guys in the school and some arseholes. Once a week we had to schlepp to some godforsaken place to play football and there was a pool. It had been closed for many years and had just reopened so the school didn't yet have a tradition for producing swimmers but were keen to at least put some chaps forward for an interschool swimming competition. And I jokingly swam for the school – I think I came about last since I hardly practised and was smoking, so I was really getting into limbo land. Until I entered that dungeon of a school, I was a very good swimmer but it had gone the way of any talent I might have had.

I did have a school chum called Morris, whom I admired. He carried himself well, like he was loved and admired at home and that gives you an aura; he wore nice jackets and shirts while I wore bum-freezers. He was not so firm a friend as I would have liked but we did hang out together although I was never invited to his home. We played truant once or twice on sports day and walked over Springfield Park. Morris had a small world of wisdom in him, obviously gleaned from a caring and attentive dad and he imparted his advice on sexual matters to me in a very mature way for someone who was just 14.

'Before you get married,' he told me, 'make sure your future wife has a proper sexual examination by a doctor as well as yourself.' I never forgot him saying that since it seemed years beyond his time but he did get married at 16 or 17! What a bright fellow he was and so very handsome with his blond hair and strong teeth. He always looked so wholesome and boy, he was strong since he had his own weights at home and was doing, so he told me, a Charles Atlas course. And he works out to this day – good old Morris!

The 'Hill' (as Stamford Hill was fondly called by its more devoted natives) was a kind of alternative school where you learned simple and more basic things to do with existence. Its grapevine was exceedingly active and so anything that went on in the world that might have some impact on you was speedily circulated – like odd jobs, schemes, how to get on to Merchant Navy ships and tour the world or see Europe working on the PX stores on American Army bases, which would take you almost every-where if you had the basic skill of knowing how to stick a tape measure up some sweaty bloke's crotch. And of course I did all of them, the Merchant Navy and the PX stores, but that was to come.

I started to go twice-weekly to a gym near Tottenham called Reuben's and I was finding a little more self-worth as I pushed the weights off my chest and fairly rapidly got up to

150 pounds. I went regularly two or three times a week and enjoyed it. It may have also saved my bacon since I had to carry my training gear in an old leather bag. I was standing up the 'Hill' one night after training, just chatting outside the milk bar when I felt a tap on my shoulder and some bloke aimed a kick directly at my future. Luckily, as I turned, I swung the bag round in front of my crotch and the slob merely kicked it and then ran off.

The villain was a troubled lunatic called Mervyn, who was the Hill's village idiot, so to speak. He was used by most aspiring young men as a warm-up bout when he was always well trounced. Obviously the poor bloke was a bit of a psycho to have even entertained such a cowardly deed, no doubt egged on by another of the psychos who hung around the 'Hill', their brains obviously in meltdown.

So a 'public' battle was arranged by the heavies for their amusement and one night in early spring, when it was still light we all walked to Clapton Pond, the scene of my earlier seminal evacuations. Suddenly a small crowd had gathered behind us to watch the event and it felt quite exciting; I found myself exhilarated. However, it turned out to be a farce since once I started (and my style was a bit of a two-hand frenzy), he didn't actually engage with me at all. The poor bum ran off! So that was that, although Moisher popped me on the eye for no good reason that I could see and I suffered a shiner for a couple of weeks. I felt no anger since it all happened so quickly and I was still so enam-oured of the '*shtarkers*' that I almost felt honoured.

As an up-and-coming nobody, these characters seemed to embody something noble and mysterious. Of course I never knew anything about them, rarely saw them anywhere else except on the 'Hill', where they stood as if they were Guardians of the Manor, which in a way they were. Moisher's mate was Ronnie of the strange sloping walk. Then there was Harry, another strange and exceedingly brutish beast, with heavy full lips and Mongolian-looking cheekbones. He was a self-declared tearaway and actually quite dangerous, with several nuts loose that might have needed tightening but he was certainly fearless. One of his hobbies was putting his fists through doors though one day he tried one that was a little too sturdy and his arm was in plaster for a few weeks. So that seemed to be the focus of these kids, to be the Princes of the Domain, the 'Guv'nors'. It was as natural as the Darwinian theory of evolution to assert themselves as the Alpha males.

Their genetic history made them what they were; it operated on them perfectly. Except when they became adults there would be no place for them apart from prison or as boxers, villains (if they were clever enough) or, as the last resort, taxi drivers – the honourable calling for working-class Jews who virtually monopolised the trade. But now these young Jewish boys were in their prime: heroic and beautiful, with thick manes of luxuriant dark hair. They demonstrated their virility in the gym or in brutal punch-ups; they were intoxicated by the drug produced out of their own bodies called sex, the euphoria of youth pounding through them. In an earlier age they might have been warriors but now they were brilliant studs who could only hang about, strut, pose, chatter idly, watch and mark their domain as if some primitive forest. Indeed, they were marking their territory, just as they once did in Odessa, Warsaw, Vienna, Berlin, Lodz… and not that long ago. A shop doorway, a wall to lean against, watching the world go by and knowing so little about it except what was in their exceedingly small one yet still feeling as if they were self-appointed generals, guarding the gates to Nowheresville. I, the watcher, the admirer, would tiptoe quietly into their shadows: this was our territory; this was us, our small kingdom.

And there was of course Nigel, who trained to be an accountant but also harboured secret desires to become a 'shtarker', who had befriended me. An interesting bloke, who always had something to say, he also possessed a weird strut but seemed consumed with an ambition to prove himself and doubtless had a lot of courage when it became necessary. Then there was 'Boxer', as he came to be known. A fascinating outsider with a large Roman nose and a thick mane of hair, he was noted as eccentric who never wore a jacket or a coat even in the most severe winters, just a T-shirt. He appeared to have a formidable physique but was a calm and unaggressive young man. Boxer loved jiving and was probably the Hill's first 'Bohemian'. Later he ended up in Paris as a busker, singing 'My Yiddisher Mama' round the Jewish areas! He did have a quite beautiful deep baritone but others less charitably disposed thought him a bit of a 'poser'. So, on the 'Hill' we were all soldiers, all members as if conscripted. Other areas had their own soldiers and armies and usually kept away, but not always.

I was blessed with many cousins, mostly on my father's side since nearly all my mother's family had fled to America, the land of the free. My lovely Auntie Mary, whom I adored and who was such a divine, warm-hearted woman, had two sons called Willie and Sidney (or just Siddy) and I really liked and admired them both. Sid was dating a bright and cheeky girl called Barbara who was from Stamford Hill. Quite often when she saw me hanging about outside the arcade she would beg me to come down East with her since she was mad about Sid and needed a young companion to go with her. I was glad to do so and so we would jump on the 653. We used to go to a little dance club, more a youth club, just off New Road, off Whitechapel.

Sid loved Barb, but Barb was just crazy about Sid, who was a tall, good-looking youth in a rough, working-class kind of way. He had a sweetness about him yet was tough as nails. Sid had little education and took odd jobs – he even worked for a chicken slaughterer at one time. But he impressed

124

Barb with his quiet, stoic confidence. His dad was called Henry, a barber, but you risked your life having your hair cut by him since his clippers always nipped you and that once was more than enough. So in the East End their hangout was outside Johnny Isaacs' famous fish and chip shop in Whitechapel – in the summer it was the place to be on a Sunday night. There was always a great crowd there.

On Sunday afternoons the ritual was to go to the Super cinema on the 'Hill' – everybody went there, no matter what kind of trash was on. You and your mate would navigate the aisles of hope, looking for a pair of nice girls to sit next to and flirt with. The girls knew this to be part of the ritual and sat there expectantly, while pretending they were there to see the film! Sid and Barb happened to be in the cinema on that fateful day when Harry, the Hill's favourite 'villain', was sitting behind them and in his usual fashion was making some kind of noise. Siddy turned and asked him to be quiet and as a payment for his impudence received a terrible blow to his face that almost knocked him out. Of course Harry couldn't help himself: when you're inclined to violence and see an opportunity at every juncture of your life, that's what you do.*

Poor Sid went home, if not to hospital but he wasn't going to take this with his tail between his legs. He waited many weeks for his bruises to heal and then went into training

---

*Whilst writing this I spoke to Sydney who now says that they actually went outside to 'settle' it. When Sid was taking off his jacket Harry struck him.

125

with my cousin Willy, his older, Ju-Jitsu trained brother. Thereafter, he issued a challenge to Harry that he would be coming up to 'see' him. Sid was only 16 whereas Harry was 18 or 19 and in those young years, that is a wide gap. Even now I cannot say how that made me feel. I was breathless, stunned, amazed my young cousin was going to take on the Hill's toughest fighter. My admiration for him was boundless, even beyond that – I worshipped the ground he walked on. Brave Sid! So that autumn Sid and Willy came up to the 'Hill' and waited for him. Sid had cut his hair short and greased it so that it couldn't be gripped but Harry never turned up. Sid waited for hours then simply took the bus back to the East End, but then turned up again the next night.

Yes, it did feel like a tale of ancient chivalry: Beowulf waiting for the Beast. Never was a young man so proud (since Sid was my bloodline) and so each night I would come up and watch the two brothers just waiting and then go home. To me it seemed strange that Harry would duck out of this one and maybe he wasn't so brave as we thought, maybe he also sensed this one would be different. He seemed invincible and nobody had ever been able to beat this tearaway with his huge fists. I was afraid for Sid since Harry could damage him badly but young, lithe Sid was waiting for him: Harry had no other recourse for Sid would not go away. He would come up every day, even for years if he had to, I suspected. One evening, several weeks later, Harry arrived with his brother and we all went behind the Super, the traditional 'testing ground' for such jousts – or rather 'killing ground'. Sex and violence took place in dark and remote corners.

Sid was not going to out-punch Harry (which would be folly), he would wrestle him to the ground – and so he did. He threw his weight against Harry and toppled him. Harry was now trapped beneath Sid, his arms pinned down. Sid took Harry's head and smashed it against the pavement. My heart was pounding, my body shaking: it seemed as if he was beating him to death. Ronnie suddenly stepped in but Willy said: 'Don't interfere, Ronnie,' and Ronnie stepped back respectfully. Meanwhile, Sid continued to whack him.

This was the punch-up to end all punch-ups. But during this onslaught when Harry was being pulverised, he actually said: 'You'd better finish me off 'cos I'll kill you if you don't,' or words very close to that. Now such words to come out of this beast impressed me deeply but Sid mercifully stopped. He had had enough and let Harry off the hook. It could have been a lot worse. Sid got up and dusted himself off. Willy, my dear cousin, actually said: 'If they bother you, let me know.' Yes, they were my divine cousins – they were heroes! My ears were ringing, my heart pounding, nothing could beat that. This was the greatest event so far of my young life and nothing would come even near to that – I shall carry it in my heart for the rest of my life. Sid did marry Barbara and she was very happy: Barbara's family took Sid into the *Shmutter* business and he became a *guntza mucker* (a big man)!

Part III

The Age of Work

Before I was quite 15, I left the mortuary that had been my school and looked for a job, having been trained to do nothing and given zero guidance, either by the moronic teachers or my own benighted parents. Like any other totally useless, skill-less piece of flesh, I studied the ads in the evening papers for a job, anything to earn money. An office job, what insanity! An office job in a dreary engineering firm off Baker Street, earning £3.10 a week, but at least I would be earning. I had not the faintest idea what I was doing or what I was supposed to be doing. As far as I was concerned this was total madness. On the first day I teamed up with a young delinquent and within the space of a lunch hour we had made a plan to do some robbery, which seemed an exciting thing to do and of course the natural conse- quence of the neglect and indifference shown me in the last years. I had become a bum, of that there was no question.

My new friend told me about a 'rich gay' who lived in Lisle Street, China Town and how we could easily rob him. That

seemed quite plausible to me, so after work we paid him a
visit. This was my first day at work and I was 15! We got to
Lisle Street and rang the doorbell whereupon we were
alarmed to be greeted by a strapping bodybuilder who must
have been his bodyguard, who had likely been hired by our
rather cautious host! We then met this rather elegant man
who was most charming to us, suspecting nothing and so we
sat and chatted while the host made us a light supper. Quite
the chef, he knocked up some delicious pasties, crisp on the
outside with cooked sweet tomatoes and onions within. He
called the dish 'Nightingale's Eyes'! And so we chatted most
pleasantly. By the end of the meal, we had quite forgotten
what we had come for and then I left to go home. Ma had
been waiting for me, wondering how my first day at work
had been. It didn't even occur to me that she would be waiting
since the world of anxious parents zealously monitoring their
child's every step meant less than nothing to me.

I wanted nothing: just to exist in a pleasant, meaningless
vacuum, obeying only some primitive instinct for survival.
What things might have motivated my spirit to stir from its
bed of sloth were denied me, no matter how I begged for
them. Even to this day it mystifies me that my own mother
who had herself been given a piano by her boxing brother
(Uncle Alf) and who had been a virtuoso pianist from early
teens could have denied my constant whine for such an
instrument, even if it was an old broken-down Joanna. She
even liked to proudly boast of how at the age of 11 she had

played for school hymns, yet when I showed some evidence of having inherited this musical gene and wished for some cheap old one, it was denied me for over 10 years; even the bike was denied me, deemed too dangerous. But what was not denied me? As if by reflex action, everything and anything, it seemed.

So eventually in the face of such obstacles, you feed on yourself and easily give way to your emotions and to others' values. Having no one at home to guide me, I was prone to be easily led by others: I would be guided by them. I wanted love and sex, often both at the same time. Sex would not be denied me, no matter how much they might have wished to deny even that. But sex as a means of escape was my goal and I would search for it without restraint, with abandon. Always searching for love, the sweet love of a woman who would give and who would take what you had to give. I worked at this meaningless job until total lack of interest led to my dismissal within a few weeks. However, one thing I never lost was my desire to read: I never lost the habit since Ma took me with her as a child and I would pick up my two books a week. But now as a young working adult I started to get acquainted with another world. I went to the youth employment agency in Oxford Street and they asked me what kind of work I wished to do and what ambitions I had so I replied 'advertising' since I had met a chap quite by chance who was a copywriter in an advertising agency and it seemed quite a romantic job to have.

As it so happened there was a job going as a messenger boy at 'Auger and Turner', a small advertising agency in Gerrard Street Soho. This had to be the lowest of the low, the real bottom of the ladder, but in some ways I enjoyed it since the staff were pleasant and somewhat creative. All I had to do was deliver the small advertising blocks to Fleet Street each day. Not only was that a doddle but I got to know all the newspapers and at the same time enjoy a brisk walk there and back. We were situated in a funky part of London and each day I could view the old hookers who had their pitch just opposite us. Since they were quite ancient boilers, how they could hook any clients, I wondered yet somehow they did. The West End was quite fascinating for a newcomer in those days and the Soho streets were lined with ladies for hire. I had luncheon vouchers, which I loved to use at the Lyons Corner House, an institution of great value but now sadly lost to us. Soon I knew the West End quite well.

It was around this time that I was actually seeing a red-haired girl called Trish, who lived in a ghastly pre-war council flat in Hackney, quite near the Hackney Marshes. She was simply an office girl, deeply romantic and virtually my first dip into that vast ocean called sex. Who knows what torments and delights await those who dare to plunge just a little deeper into its infernal depths? What a wonderful, sexy girl she was, quite awesome, in fact. She had deep blue eyes, red hair and a delightful soft body with the one drawback that she was actually mentally uncomplicated. I was 15 and she was 17 and a virgin.

I recall one night while we were having a squeeze up against the wall of her council block actually asking her to be my 'girlfriend' – how mawkish I was then. I think she was fairly enthusiastic about the idea and so we went out together but not like a lot of young people do by introducing her to mates or your family, or doing foursomes for dinner. For us, it was just the two of us. For our nocturnal explorations we walked over to Hackney Marshes, situated conveniently behind the old pre-war council flat she lived in and found a nice grassy place to lie down out of sight of one and all. She would try to give me a 'hand-shandy' but it was quite difficult at first as she was still learning and we needed a little lubrication. At last we found a partial solution: she'd run her fingers through my hair, which was well-greased and thick in those young, horny days and we were both delighted with our biological progress.

From then on I would telephone her frequently and beetle down to Hackney. I now had something of a romance in my life. One day I was invited into her home and I must confess I had seen little like it in my life. The poor sweet girl lived in something out of Dickens or the *Elephant Man* – the flat actually stank of lard and grease while her mother was afflicted with a terrible disorder that caused her legs to swell monstrously. Her brother was a thin, sickly-looking delinquent and her father completely indifferent. So I couldn't wait to take her down to the marshes and after months of loving and squeezing, we managed to achieve our ultimate goal. She was deflowered and seemed to be as happy as I was.

From then on we discovered the phenomenal joys our entwined bodies could give us, so we did it at every possible time – in fact, incessantly. She was always there for me, adored me without restraint and loved our passion so much; and was there for me whenever my organ arose from the pit. However I was beginning to tire of her and her sweet nothings and simplicity, her total lack of any concept of the world in which we lived since for her, I was that world. She never seemed to read anything, just to exist for romance and our torrential encounters. I actually started to resent her since I felt compelled to see her merely to slake my lust, but then since we had little to say to each other, I couldn't wait to get away.

Sometimes we actually did go out and I remember taking her to see Johnny Ray, the American singer and my hero, at the London Palladium. That was a special evening and we both dressed for it. One day at the street market in Hackney she treated me to a shirt with my favourite Johnny Ray collar, a large rollaway much-favoured by louche Hollywood stars. I even took her to my home once when nobody was there but my sister came in, which surprised me. So I introduced her, feeling at the same time a bit awkward although she was pleasant and then Trisha and I left. I suppose I was venturing out of my own local environment since there were so many nice girls around my area, but with Trish there were no complications and no demands.

I tried to avoid seeing her so much, to see other girls but somehow I always came back to her. Or we might go and see a local flick and have a coat over our laps, our dancing hands be-bopping in each other's thighs. At the same time I discovered Grey's Dance Academy in Finsbury Park, a jive club and I was becoming far more adept with the jive steps, which I really adored. After the initial phase when you keep turning the poor girl round and round (which she obeyed so obediently, like a trusty horse), you picked up some more steps until you could execute amazing twists and turns and drape her arm round your neck, but the main object was to be really cool and certainly not like those raging Dixieland idiots. Sweet Trish really could not jive all that well and so I often went by myself. I had found something and that became my first love: I was a dancer. Now was the time to venture up West.

I first got to know the magic world called 'West End' when Ma would take me as a kid and the West End wasn't the sleaze pit it is today. In those days you actually wore a suit to go 'up West' – it certainly wasn't crawling with the horrors of McDonald's and Kentucky Fried Chicken. I don't know how the powers that be let it become so rancid.

In the early days for a special treat, Ma and me would take the 15 from Commercial Road and breathe a sigh of relief when the bus left Aldgate and the East End's filthy effluvium. Then just off Leicester Square was the magnificent Lyons Corner House, which was nothing less than an extraordinary cornucopia of delights with different restaurants on each floor and an extraordinary shopping deli at ground level. There was a salad bar on the first floor, where for three shillings and sixpence you could pile your plate like a small mountain. Of course that was exactly what I did, although I could never finish it – just the sheer joy of piling your plate high was irresistible. I think Ma got more pleasure from it than me since she beamed at my audacity and shared my happiness.

Sometimes we would go to the London Palladium when the superstars from America performed there and of course we would have to visit the stage door, where Ma would encourage me to shove my way in with my precious autograph book – she was always doing that. In fact, I was more of a companion to Ma than my dad, who took her nowhere. But there was a West End I never knew about, a place of wild and weird secrets, strange clubs crawling with the serpents of the underworld.

One day my mate Harold introduced me to the wonders of The Lyceum. Wow, what a place! It was the biz and the dancing was the best to be seen in London.

≡>◆<≡

Lyceum

I never knew that the place where I so eagerly improved my jiving and even at 15 was so familiar with, had been a theatre until I was informed by a kindly gentleman who visited me in a remand home (where I was shortly scheduled to continue my education!). There had been a theatre on that site since 1809 until it was destroyed by fire in 1830. The present theatre was built under the name Royal Lyceum and English Opera House in 1834. It was designed by Samuel Beazley and cost £40,000. For almost three decades the great actor-manager Henry Irving ran the place, with Bram Stoker as his company manager and advanced the art of theatre beyond any person before him or even since. Irving was smart enough to open with a crowd-pleasing melodrama called The Bells, *which became an instant hit and played to sell-out crowds for 150 nights. His greatest triumph however, was in* Hamlet, *which ran for 200 nights. Irving took over full management of the theatre in 1878. He also continued to act there until 1902, engaging actress Ellen Terry for that 24-year period also! Bram Stoker worked for Irving for 20 years and many believe Irving was the real-life inspiration for the character of Count Dracula in his 1897 novel.*

The theatre was rebuilt again in 1904 and only retained the façade and portico of the old building. In 1939 the London County Council bought the building and even planned to demolish the fantastic edifice for road widening! Luckily those plans collapsed and after the war it was converted into a huge ballroom: The Lyceum, as I knew it. The ghastly forces of the GLC again wanted to demolish it in 1968, but this time the protest was so strong that it led to the abandonment of the scheme. In 1996 the theatre was restored to full glory. Bravo!

———◆◈◆———

The Lyceum was a strange, beautiful building with giant Greek columns on the outside that lent it the grandeur of a temple. That of course was what it was, a grand temple of the arts although I was not to know that at the time. For me it was London's numero uno dance hall: you climbed the stairs, paid for your ticket and entered that great ballroom, where once were velvet seats with backsides on them watching Sir Henry Irving and Ellen Terry. Now it was Ted Heath's Band and a bunch of Teddy Boys and Girls, but these were no ordinary Teddy Boys. The craze was in, a curious throwback to the Edwardian era (hence Teddy), and in the best sense it was a super-elegant period when young chaps had their suits made with longer-than-usual jackets to accommodate at least four buttons on the front, cuffs on the sleeves, a velvet collar (almost de rigueur) and narrow, drainpipe legs on the pants; also stiff collars (separate of course from the shirts) and double cuffs. Dressed to this format, the Teddy Boys looked the biz, but there was a kind of sub-sect (whom we called 'peasants' from suburbia), who wore thick creeper shoes, soft, large-collared shirts and shoestring ties.

The jive was becoming more elegant, more complex and it was a statement of your skill and prowess. Above all, it was 'cool' unlike those mawkish idiot students leaping up and down in roll-neck sweaters, looking like the morons they were. Jive was also a class apart. Our Gods were Stan Kenton, Dave Brubeck, Duke Ellington, Count Basie, Milt Jackson Quartet, Chet Baker and George Shearing. There were some really great dancers there and the trick was to learn as many intricate ways of connecting with your partner as possible. And then you might take your 'bird' upstairs on the balcony for a drink at one of the small tables. Near the band and on the left side sat the 'faces', the 'in' crowd, the 'tearaways', but I was nowhere in their league and so I would meekly peep over from time to time to check out what female delights were on hand to pull that night. The key nights of the week were Saturdays and Sundays, but I would also go to the Sunday tea dance where they played records and dance my head off. Afterwards I'd go with a couple of mates to the Lyons Corner House on Coventry Street, change my sweat-soaked shirt for a spare that I always brought with me, wash and brush up, then 1 was ready for the night. Those were the nights when the London world was at the 'Ly', as we used to call it.

The king of the West End dance hall was appropriately called 'Curly King'. A short, colourful character with peculiar staring, rat-like eyes, a wolfish face and a large mop of hair, he seemed utterly fearless and was admired and respected by all. He was feared by all too, especially me since fear was my middle name at that young roseate time. Just to look at this creature filled one with a strange sense of awe as if he had come from the bowels of the earth, where evil gremlins lurk. He was surrounded by his adoring acolytes, but one night to my astonishment I saw my old friend from Stamford Hill, Ginger Paul, sitting there posing as some kind of *shtarker*. I guess this not-very-brave chump desperately wanted to be thought of as a bit of a villain so they let him hang around for laughs and because he was so handsome – so he was good window dressing for them.

The Krays made occasional visits but it was Curly who was definitely chief rooster. He loved to socialise and had quite a sense of humour. Only later did I discover he was, in fact, the Krays' gofer and minder! I could never mix within their circles and quite frankly, I had no desire to since my interest was merely to jive well and find the occasional romance. Invariably, the evening would end in a punch-up since for Curly this was almost a rite of passage on a weekly scale.

Pulling 'talent', as it was called then, was more difficult in the West End since the girls came from all over London, particularly south London, so opportunities were scarce. I do recall pulling a few though most times after the dance Harold and I would go to the 24-hour café upstairs at Joe Lyons Corner House on The Strand and hang about for another hour or so of idle chatter, tea and a smoke and generally have a bit of fun before jumping on the all-night bus that left from Trafalgar Square.

If it came nearly full and you couldn't get on, there was a real sigh and a gasp for you'd have to wait another hour or start to leg it! This was when I went to the Oxford Street Youth Labour Exchange and got the job as messenger boy in Gerrard Street. Now I was developing into a bit of a low-life and a thief, which never seemed to me to be too grave a sin. If your 'owners' fail to give you moral training or guidance and just let you idle along with your life, drifting along in whatever stream you are pulled to, naturally you will fall into a kind of entropy where the low lives around exert an almighty influence since your page is clear to be written on and the wrong writing can so easily be put there! So it was that I was trained by another thief in the art of nicking bikes and where to flog them, which was the Saturday market in Dalston, east London.

I believe we did it twice and it was a bit of a thrill to have an extra fiver in my hands. Anyway, I was always desperate for cash since my £3.10 didn't go too far and naturally, I had to give my mum £1.10 out of that for my keep. So, to cut a long story short, one day on my messaging hikes around Fleet Street I noticed quite an elegant bike parked near the newspaper office of the *Daily Mirror* – would you believe it but in those balmy days in Britain, few people ever locked their bikes!

So the very next time I saw it, I just got on it and cycled home. No questions asked – 'No, Mum, I just borrowed it.'

The next day I had been looking forward to spending some time with a new girlfriend I'd been seeing lately, who shared a flat with some friends. I dressed real smart in a pair of black barathea pants (the one thing given to me by Dad), a red shirt and a black-and-white hound's-tooth jacket. It was a Saturday. That afternoon I had taken my bike to the same market, where I met the man who had bought the previous nicked bike. He looked at me and the bike then said yes, he'd like to have it, but business was slow and if I was to come to his house later that night, he would give me a fiver for it.

Being a greedy fool, although I did smell a rat the lure of money and the freedom it gave masked it somewhat. After all, he had bought a bike from me before so surely there would be no problem? Like an idiot I began the fateful trek to his house. Also, I had left the bike with him at the market, which added a bit of weight to my need to see him. I knocked on the door of a small house somewhere in the grey wastelands of Hackney, he opened it and showed me into the lounge, whereupon two plainclothes cops walked into the room and bam, I was nicked! And I tell you it was the most horrible feeling of my young life. I felt my whole world collapse in front of me and at that dreadful moment my life felt dead. They shoved me into a car and drove me to the Hackney Police Station.

Now I was scared shitless and naive enough to think that when I begged them not to tell my dad, if only they had said, 'OK, son, you're free just this time but if you do it

144

again, it's jail for a year', had they given me just one slim chance, just a whisper of forgiveness then I would never have stolen anything again. But alas, such hopes are only in our dreams. No, the full awful, ugly weight of the Law had to be unleashed on my head, which was destined to turn young boys like me into criminals, social misfits with horrendous mental issues. Naturally, they called home and shortly afterwards Dad came storming in like 'Stormin' Norman' and he actually went to take a crack at me. And the cops had to hold him back. What a complete and utter bastard! I would have welcomed just the smallest bit of compassion but no, just an outburst from all the hate and loathing that he obviously felt for me. He drove me home without incident, no doubt after a warning from the Law.

Mum behaved calmly and sympathetically and made me a lovely breakfast-in-bed of fried tomatoes on toast as if she sensed it might be my last for a while. In the morning Dad drove me to the Juvenile Court in Commercial Street in the East End. For this occasion, I had changed my clothes to something more sombre but kept on the same black pants that Dad had actually made for another customer who hadn't shown up. We all thought I would no doubt get probation since this was really my first-known offence. However, I wasn't to know that I would be facing a deeply unsympathetic character called Basil Henriques, much-admired for his public services and better-known still for his passion in sending young boys to Borstal.

Without much ado I was remanded for two weeks for examination before sentencing, as if this sentence wasn't enough. However, having seen so many movies from Hollywood about jails, it all seemed a bit of an exciting adventure. I was duly carted off to Stamford House in Shepherd's Bush, the first rung on the ladder that for most youngsters would be a career in crime.

Stamford House was a grim Victorian institution and I arrived early afternoon in time for tea and a wedge of bread with some kind of paste. I changed into the prison grey and was put into a long dormitory, where I would be woken each morning with a jolly 'Hands off your cocks and pull up your socks!' The day was spent mainly hanging around outside in the yard or kicking a ball around since most of us were on remand for examination and judgment as to suitability for sentencing. Twice a week we'd all march to the local pool. For the first time I saw how evil some kids could be, although there were also some very interesting ones there, who were just a bit confused. Meanwhile my own life was being predetermined and taking a distinctly strange direction.

Soon my turn came to be examined by a psychiatrist as most of the kids were and I spent some time over two or three sessions with a young and most pleasant man, who proceeded to ask me about my life. He really was the first man that I could ever talk to and confide in, so I poured my heart out to him about my strange and warped life up to that point. He listened with real concern and understanding – he was the first person with whom I felt real human contact; in fact he was the first *real* human being I had spoken to since my time in New York. I felt so liberated after each session. If only all kids had this opportunity to talk, to confess, to bare their souls. Every school should have a guiding light such as this to whom troubled youngsters can unload their grief.

So he listened and confessed how amazed, if not appalled, he was by the story I told him. He found it highly significant there was a total lack of communication, let alone encouragement from my father. This, he felt, was a key to my subsequent criminality. I had no guidance either from him or from school and so consequently I had fallen into the maelstrom. He said he had witnessed many like me, who without moral guidance or help had not developed a conscience or awareness. When he told me that I obviously possessed a high intelligence and a healthy curiosity about the world, he made me glow. I told him how much I loved to read and of my desire to be something in the world, either an actor or a writer. He assured me that he would make a report recommending that I received probation and guidance; that I was a lost soul and needed and craved help, not incarceration.

He was so loving that I felt totally at peace about what I had told him about Dad and how I couldn't remember if he had taken me out more than two or three times in my entire life, but I begged that it should not be revealed in court with my dad sitting there. He assured me it would be read in confidence only by the judge.

The two weeks passed except for an altercation with some really evil kid whom I was forced to clip, but the episode was passed over.

Before the end of my stay, a person of my faith – a Jewish social worker or even a young rabbi – came to see me. They trawl these places and minorities are given the opportunity for spiritual comforting. He spoke to me sympathetically and thus became the second man in my life to whom I could pour out my woes. He asked what kind of things I liked to do and I said I liked dancing and that one of my favourite places was The Lyceum Dance Hall in The Strand. And then he said something that for some reason I have never forgotten, as if it struck some ancient bell with a giant thwack. He merely told me that The Lyceum, which of course I only knew as a dance hall, used to be a theatre years ago. I paid little attention to that comment at the time except to register surprise since I had no idea my favourite dance hall was once a theatre, yet something moved in the reptilian area of my brain. That comment stayed in my mind and to this day, I recall him saying it to me.

After two weeks I was driven back to the Toynbee Juvenile Court with the report from the psychoanalyst that I would no doubt get probation and supervision – and that of course no mention would be made of our conversations about my father in an open court.

So I stood before this great old slob and he actually humiliated me by quoting chunks of my private confession regarding Dad. I was never so embarrassed. Then he also had to hand a report from Baulk, the crusty old headmaster of Grocer's School, who actually recommended I be sent away! The dear old sod had probably never forgotten or got over the incident of the boy who refused to bend down like some dumb slave and be whacked. The school that I had entered with such passion and optimism had crushed the life and joy from me. Having failed me grotesquely, it now sought to bang the final nail in the coffin. Without more ado I was sentenced to three months in a detention centre.

The most disgusting part of the whole proceedings was when the old slug casually tossed a few snippets out from the 'confidential' report my nice psychiatrist had drawn up for me. He just tossed them off like an afterthought and it was not only deeply humiliating but utterly destructive: I felt as if I had died in that court.

Now as it so happens my beloved Dad had brought me a spare pair of trousers – he needed the beautiful black barathea pants back since obviously the customer must have turned up. So I went into the men's toilet and changed, then

149

gave him back my, or rather his, black pants. In front of me he examined them and just had to make some vile comment – he couldn't have just thrown them in the bag and had them dry-cleaned. No, that would be beyond him.

So, glad to get away from him, from the family, from Manor House, I was taken off in a car to Paddington Station, then to Oxford. I was curious about the new life being shaped around me without me lifting a finger: the world was absorbing me in its system with only the slightest aid from me. By now I was starving and when we hit Oxford I was treated to a ham sandwich and a tea at the cafeteria. Shortly afterwards a car arrived to take me to my new home for the next three months.

⟫⟨

Campsfield House, Kidlington, Oxford

In the early-1950s a group of enlightened criminal authorities devised an institution called the 'detention centre', the cruel successor to Borstal training/youth custody. The centres were a new kind of experiment designed to administer a 'short, sharp shock' aimed to deter future young criminals from the inevitable path. They were meant to be a form of concentration camp, using a regime of strict rules, harsh discipline, punishment and ball-breaking physical work whereas in truth they actually helped destroy young lives, with plenty of evidence of inmates suffering casual brutality. Not surprisingly, the system modelled on negativity and mindless routine eventually proved to be a failure. Sadly, unimaginative magistrates dispatched hordes of young people to these hell-houses, where they suffered beyond their wildest dreams. They were altogether hopeless places, manned by sadistic bullies, with no possibility of redemption.

Kidlington was its dull and unassuming name. The detective with whom I had such a pleasant chat on the journey marched me into the Governor's office and when I failed to punctuate my speech with 'Sirs', the Governor himself began screaming in such a way that I really thought he must be insane: 'Say "Sir" when you answer me!' Immediately, I threw a glance at the detective as if to say, 'Help, take me out of this madhouse!' but he could only glance back sympathetically, say nothing and then he left. I imagine the loony was trying to get me in the mood but the only emotions he inspired were utter contempt and disgust.

I always seemed to arrive at these places for teatime so I was given a lukewarm bath, got into my grey prisoner outfit and marched down to tea. There I sat with a group of kids, also newly arrived and we all chatted furiously, even giggled our heads off. Then we were locked in our cells. Everyone had their own narrow cell for the first week and then you went into the dorm with the other louts. You were woken early and had to do everything on the double, military fashion. But first your bed must be perfectly made up, perfect ship-shape, with sharp hospital corners. This was inspected and then you ran down for breakfast – basic slop food but with a rather nice cocoa. After this you were given a job but first we were all lined up outside for an indeterminate time before being allocated our dreary duties.

Fortunately I only had to clean toilets and scrub floors for the simple reason I developed a hernia (if not two), my injuries were caused by Leese, the ruthless PT master. I could never forget his cruel, cold-eyed face – he was the most sadistic human I had ever come across. One of his favourite devices was to get you to run around the gym with a log held out in front of you, then run or do knee bends until you dropped from exhaustion whereupon you would be struck for your feebleness.

PT meant fear, the worst fear imaginable. I imagine the louts who devised this system thought it would terrify us into never coming back but it only made the tough boys harder, the weaker ones suicidal. We had this after a day's work as the completion to each day. Once a week we had sweet rations, which were looked forward to with an insane passion. At 6pm we were all marched into a large room to listen to the news. After it finished the guard would point at one of us and then the prisoner would have to remember some part of the news. He would then point at the next and so forth. After a few responses it became harder and harder to find a crumb of news that hadn't already been chewed up but it certainly made you listen to what was going on in the world. Being a bit of an alert chap, I carefully picked out some obscure bits of news and was always able to come up with something. You were then returned to your cell and the next day was a replica of the one before.

We ate our meagre rations with great care, chewing the portions immensely slowly, dreading the moment when we'd devoured the last crumb. It was only with enormous willpower that I was able to sacrifice a slice of bread to my starving colleagues for a half-bar of chocolate on sweets day and so on one day I would well and truly feast. However, that 'willpower' was my undoing since the kid with whom I had traded actually avoided paying me for my endeavours. I was caught demanding payments but so suddenly was the screw there that I now realise I must have been set up.

The creepy little screw almost licked his thin lips like a lizard as he grinned and said: 'Ah! Now we have our first sweet baron!' Hardly a baron, I would have thought, but for this *serious* offence I was put in solitary confinement for seven days. It was a punishment that I don't think I ever recovered from since you were alone, all alone, night and day – and if there was anything I loathed more than anything, it was being left alone. But there I was, and to pass the time I was given rusty metal trays to scrape. For my morning treat, I was made to run naked and wash under a freezing-cold shower. The odd thing was that after the shower, I actually felt the wintry prison air to be nice and warm.

Now if the adult world wasn't so full of delinquent opinions they might have used the opportunity to talk to me, to guide me, to train me, to find out what had gone wrong in my life to bring me to this pretty pass, to teach me… anything! Instead the slugs kept me in an unheated cell all day, alone and scraping tins. What effect they thought this might have on me, I don't know but I do know it embittered me and sowed a rage inside that would never be depleted.

It's a strange thing to be put into solitary confinement at 15 years old – and for what? It's an act of madness perpetrated against a defenceless person by lunatics sanctioned by the state, who think they are doing society some good when all they needed to do was to communicate with you: just listen and talk. But this is the one thing they are utterly incapable of: they don't know how to, they haven't a clue what it means to communicate with a young person. So this is their talk: violence against someone who is basically still a child, vulnerable to the schemes and machinations of others. So for those moronic toe-rags of the state their communication was to put me in a cold cell all day, scraping rusty baking trays with nothing to read, nothing to listen to, so a day is divided into looking forward to breakfast, lunch and dinner, with scrape, scrape, scrape in between.

I shall never forget the nights when I just stared out of the window and saw the lights in the distance as cars came and went. I started to wonder if I would ever get out, maybe they would just keep me there as long as they wished. As the headlights slowly passed on the distant road, I wondered about who was driving and envied their ability just to go into a shop and buy a chocolate bar. How wonderful it must be out there, how amazing freedom must be.

Since it was December the nights came early and I could just lay in the dark and think. I had much to think about and I would lay in the dark and go over everything in my life. Often I'd dream about my time in New York and yearn to be back there. I had a recurring dream when I'd be walking in The Bronx, where Uncle Joe had his ramshackle rooming house and I couldn't find the way yet somehow I knew I was not far, but I could never find it. I'd ask strangers for help and directions. I wasn't unhappy in the dream since at least I was in my beloved country but I just couldn't find my home there.

We were allowed to write home once a week and I recall writing to ask how Dad was and if the shop was doing OK. When I got out, my mother actually said the most ridiculous thing I ever heard her say, which was: 'You wrote asking how many orders Dad had taken because you knew it would be read by the guards.' I then thought how poor deluded, simple-minded Mum and me were a thousand worlds apart; that even if Dad had treated me like a piece of shit for as long as I could remember, I still had an innate instinct to wish to bond with him, as all sons do.

In fact he visited me just the once in three months. Mum couldn't come since she had been desperately ill and confined to hospital, where a very good surgical team rescued her from almost certain death after a burst appendix. Naturally I'd think about Ma and how my arrest and incarceration may have contributed to her illness. This, above everything else, filled me with such a terrible guilt and resolved in me a strong desire never to do anything that would land me in such hell again.

My sister never visited either, not once. I expect she was too busy looking after and worrying about our mother. And when Dad did come, I couldn't talk – I could only cry during the half-hour he had with me. He tried to hand me a bag of sweets but the warden said it wasn't allowed. It was a terrible moment. He attempted to jostle me with his trilby hat but I just couldn't control myself and that was the last time I saw him there. He came only that once but it was the first and only time that I saw true feeling and sorrow in his eyes and I loved him for it. Nobody else came and to tell you the truth, I didn't miss my family nor did it occur to me to want to see anyone else in that place.

On Christmas day I was let out to mix with the other inmates during the daytime, which was a real treat for me, but at the end of the day I was put back in my solitary cell. I heard another boy who was in the next cell, I heard sounds like people shouting, or at least he was shouting. When I heard his voice, I knew who the boy was: he was one of the tougher kids in there and he was shouting at one of the piggy-eyed warders, who I also found to be a particularly repellent slug. 'No, I won't take me shoes off!' he was shouting. Obviously the slug was aching to beat him but was afraid of those heavy-duty boots we had to wear. Then it was silent and I heard the fat slug slither away, unfulfilled.

Eventually came the day of my release and I was so excited, I could barely sleep. Though I woke early, no one came to release me. I imagined all kinds of scenarios and had a terrible and irrational fear the filthy scum would keep me there. Few people knew where I was or were able to fight my case for me and so I prayed. I prayed so hard: I prayed that I would never do anything bad again, that I would not associate with any of the boys I had met there and made friends with. The hours dripped away painfully slowly. Eventually the door opened and then the guard came in and told me to get ready to go. And that was it: there was no farewell, not even from the assistant governor, who had befriended me – nothing, only that blast of fresh air.

Oh, the sheer pleasure I took in putting on my nice soft clothes and my smart gabardine coat that I treasured. I was taken to the station by one of the most sadistic guards, whose rough red face and dirty reddish hair always gave him the appearance of an angry ogre, but he behaved normally and I did not have one word to say to him. Once there, I was given a ticket and got on the train. There was such a strange sensation of suddenly sitting on soft seats and looking at normal, nice commuters on their way to London, reading the morning papers that I found it quite lyrical. I had been told Dad would meet me at Paddington Station but since I did not immediately see him, I was in no mood to wait and so I jumped on the tube and went to my home in Manor House. Our nice little flat looked really very shabby and neglected since Mum was still in hospital and so the first thing I did was to start cleaning, something I had now been well trained for.

I didn't leave the flat for a week and saw no one: I just sat and felt sorry for myself – ashamed, though not for the crime but the sheer pettiness of it. How could I go to Stamford Hill and show my face? Had I stolen a car or broken in somewhere then I might have had a vestige of pride but for pilfering a mere bike… This was what children do.

I wondered how many of them would know for I had suddenly disappeared. But I am sure the word went round and they had seen it in a local paper. At last I fancied getting my arms round my girlfriend, so I rang Trisha and arranged on Saturday night to meet her at the Royal Tottenham to re-emerge slowly into society.

'Where you been, Les?' asked my mates, with the suggestion of a grin.

'Oh, just staying with my sister in Hastings, 'cos Mum was ill and all that.'

'Oh, [smirk, smirk] you been with your sister in Hastings? Oh yeah? Right!'

(Beryl always found the most outlandish places to live like Hastings, Totnes and Gloucester, then always pined for London and yet never moved there.) The ribbing soon passed and I was happy to taste some female flesh again.

Soon I found another dead-end job in St Martin's Lane. It lasted a few weeks only I didn't have a vague idea of what I was doing. From the age of 15, one job drifted into another with no sense of purpose, no ambition and no desire other than to earn wages and fill in the great yawning days, just to leave the house in the morning and come home at night. Then at night to go out, to go dancing, slink around the West-End small clubs, find a girl, seek out some comfort and thrills, to get home, get up, go to work again and watch the years slowly grind past. 'The Wasteland', it might be

159

called, but I did have an agenda, a childish fantasy that in some way I would do something important, I would become known, become famous and therefore could I not mark time until I saw the road along which I must travel?

So that was my agenda: I was determined to be famous but famous for something worthwhile, the nature of which had so far evaded me and I had no idea why I suffered from this ridiculous and obsessive desire. Maybe it was a reaction to the barren lands I had been wandering through for the last five years; perhaps I was determined to achieve some form of compensation. I would make something of my life – but how? So in the simple mindset of limited choices, I thought I would one day attempt to be a movie actor. Childish perhaps, but for that dumb-arse occupation (although I didn't quite see it like that then), I had all the right qualifications: legs, arms, eyes and hair, plus a mouth and a tongue. What more could you need?

Many movie actors are plucked off the streets. They are only one degree higher than those who are unkindly considered the lowest of mortals: models. But instead of modelling clothes or poisonous unguents, they are modelling a few words – except of course those who really have studied the craft or have other techniques such as singing and dancing. But for every Gene Kelly, you have 50 Jayne Mansfields. However, that was my distant dream, which made it possible for me to amble along, just for now. All this trudging and hustling was merely preparation and the thought in the back of my mind made it possible for me to keep going.

And keep going I did: from bad to worse and even worst. I once ended up in an East-End confectionery wholesaler's: that was pretty boring and all I can remember is the lugging backwards and forwards and the incredibly early hours of work. I even worked in a button shop in the Commercial Road, which was the absolute nadir of my life but most of the jobs lasted a week, sometimes even less.

Eventually I applied for a job in one of the most beautiful small shops in London, called W. Bill, of South Molton Street, W1. It was a very high-class cashmere house and also sold high-quality British cloth so in a way I was more in my old element. South Molton Street is an elegant tributary running off the poisonous cesspit of Oxford Street but it is a world of exclusive fashion and antiquity. It was a pleasure just to walk down it, as it even is today. I was interviewed by the very charming manageress (Miss Shepherd), a middle-aged woman who showed me around and described how some of the colours in the gorgeous sweaters were the natural colour of the goat whence they came. Ah! I was actually learning something. Something switches on in my brain whenever information comes in. I was able to conceal my recent incarceration and present myself as a worthy young man.

I got the job and each day I would take the tube – Manor House on the Piccadilly Line to Holborn, change onto the Central Line to Bond Street. Then I was actually given a beautiful slipover to wear in the shop and of course, take home. I was simply overjoyed. Life was beginning to take a much more rosier turn. At the far end of the shop was a real fireplace. It was kept going by an old warehouse-type bloke and all the staff were women who were refined and elegant, who sat behind desks since there were no ghastly shop counters.

Suddenly my life took on a sea change you might say, for now I was elegantly dressed in a pinstriped suit I had paid my dad to make and felt most refined. I was so happy there in that beautiful and elegant street, made friends with assistants in the neighbouring shops and joined the community. Each day I proudly wore my soft cashmere slipover, which cost a fortune (at least £40 and this was half a century ago!). However, they never seemed short of customers and I saw Ava Gardner in there one day, but I was not allowed to serve the clientele: I was there to stand around, run errands, arrange the stock and poke the fire. One of my joys was to collect suit samples from Savile Row for customers looking for Donegal tweed, worsteds or barathea. And so gradually I began to acquire knowledge of retailing and textiles. I swiftly made friends with all the lovely middle-aged dowagers who worked there and I believe they found me most congenial. In hindsight, I realise they must have been a small lesbian community.

It was a very pleasant Radclyffe Hall, if that is appropriate and they were all so charming and friendly that for the first time in my life I felt totally at ease with the world and even looked forward to going to work. I conveyed as much at home as I entertained Mum with stories about the life of this unique store and its clients and how special and charming my employers were to me.

Now I had a sister with whom I had one of those normal relationships, which was an unspoken code to keep out of my life since she had this rather strange habit of interfering somewhat. And it was Beryl, maybe guided by Mum, who put a stop to that very special relationship I had with Shirley, which started when I was 10 and whom I adored. Of this I have not the slightest doubt and it gave me the first shock of guilt that we were doing something that had to be stopped since it was unwholesome. It led the way to realising unwholesome relationships, which brought about the sad situation with Trisha and the pregnancy, of more shortly. It may be fanciful to cite this event as being the first blow that reverberated right through my early teens but I blamed her for the rest of my life.

One day, and to my absolute horror, a horror of a kind one cannot easily imagine, I saw my sister enter W. Bill – my sanctuary, my home, my own individual, special space. I saw her enter the shop and be interviewed at the desk by the manageress. I think I may have mentioned they were looking for a replacement and without once asking if I would mind, without telling me a thing, she had the sheer gall to enter this private world of mine, the envelope of my security. She had not the remotest regard for my feelings or my person; it was as if I didn't exist. It was one of those blows to my ego and to my world that I would never forget, ever – these things stay in your mind for a long time.

Even to this day I can see her sitting there in the shop, in *my* shop, while I stood and sweated with shame. My feelings had not the slightest effect on the total absorption of her own needs and I loathed her with a loathing quite murderous. Although the hate fortunately subsided, the dull bruising remains to this day, along with a catalogue of other events or 'liberties' taken, as we used to call them in those days. Needless to say, she didn't get the job since obviously they didn't want a 'family' there and she certainly wasn't the type of English 'rose' they were looking for. Beryl was not unat-tractive, though and possessed my father's dark, saturnine colouring with chestnut hair and deep brown eyes, which made her look more Greek or Italian. Eventually my 'enmity' faded and we sort of became friends again.

Just about this time when, for the very first time in my life I was finding some degree of happiness and joy, an interest in something beyond my own needs, the bomb dropped. Trisha, that sweet, clueless flower from Hackney in whom I used to pour my libations with relentless regularity (and without a condom since it was confiscated by my enlightened mother) became pregnant. Instead of praising me for my wisdom and stressing how important it was to use birth control whenever the opportunity arose, alas no such wise advice was forthcoming. Unfortunately or rather stupidly, I then associated condoms with some dirty pornographic thing and so this happened. What a dysfunctional family we were!

So, all sex was pushed under the carpet as well as love, comfort and cheer and my sweet Shirley. Poor Trisha cried and squealed and we got pills, she took hot baths, swallowed gin and went to the doctor's, but all to no avail – that kid was well and truly cemented in. So, for seven months of my life, since she was two months gone when she confessed her pregnancy to me, I had to live with it. And so I spent each day in a state of anxiety and fear. I even tried to do something myself since the street knowledge was that if you inserted a douche pipe with some soapy water into the womb it would abort the baby, but if you got air into it then you might kill the mother. After a messy start, we gave up on that one. I became severely depressed and the change in me was so obvious that I lost my job with W. Bill and was in Palookaville once again.

Sadly, though I really couldn't stand the girl anymore I was drawn back by the easy availability of the drug of sex, which was all I managed to do. She was very romantic and dreamed of us getting a little flat by putting our wages together and we would live happily ever after, but such an idea was anathema to me. And I was hardly even shaving yet.

Eventually the thing popped out and quite naturally, she took me to court to sue for maintenance. With the help of a completely useless solicitor I made a half-hearted effort to deny it was mine and was subsequently clobbered with a court order to pay what amounted to nearly a third of my wages each week. Trisha was overjoyed, even a mite surprised at the amount and made a rather kindly deal that if I would visit the homestead once a week she would give me back half, which was quite sweet of her. However, those Sunday visits were horrors I would never forget since I had not the slightest paternal feelings. I was now 16 and the wretched, wailing thing didn't seem to be anything to do with me. She would hand me the brat, insisting I hold her, and that was the very worst of all. I don't know why I felt this revulsion but I did: I almost felt sick and was glad to hand it back to her.

Trisha was so very happy with her little one, whom I believe she called 'Tina'. But now, over the years, my memory may be a little faulty. I could see how Trisha had suffered over the last months and how she came through with flying colours while I was the dark and dirty villain. After a while my visits grew less but the payment still had to be met and if I dropped them for more than a couple of weeks there would be a knock on the door from a grey-faced man from the court threatening police action and sometimes my blessed Ma paid up for me. Dad never found out, thank God, since the repercussions would be too horrible to imagine. However, the good news was that Trisha eventually married a builder with whom she dropped a couple more kids and I was relieved of the everlasting payments.

In fact, four years later when I became a student for the first time in my life and won a small scholarship to drama school, I applied to have my payments stopped since she had married. Well, the upshot of this was that the court agreed but one day I had a visit from the 'husband'. More full of hate and aggression than anyone I had hitherto seen, he arrived at the door. He had come to get me to sign an agreement to wipe my name off the child's birth certificate, or rather for a change of name to his. To do this we had to go to a Justice of the Peace. When he visited our flat, I couldn't help but feel somewhat violated even though what he felt was probably justified by the stories he must have heard from Trisha. I remember that I couldn't even bring him in the living room, which was my mum's pride and joy and so we sat in the kitchen, where he verbally abused me roundly. We found a Justice of the Peace and signed the various papers then he left and of course I neither saw nor heard from him again. I often wonder how Trisha and my daughter are and what they are doing and how their lives have turned out.

Having been sacked from W. Bill, I felt I had at least raised my status in the world and so I sought another West-End job. I found a salesman's job with Harry Fisher, shirt maker, of Upper Regent Street, W1. It was a small, very elegant shop, about a hundred yards from the BBC. Apart from the thick tosser whom he employed as a sub-manager, Harry was a gem of a man – a rare, gentle, fatherly figure – and I really liked him. The shop continually stank of the Mannequin cigars he used to smoke though nobody seemed to mind in those tolerant, far-off days. He was popular with the moneyed classes, who would have their shirts made to measure, with beautiful cutaway collars and you always knew a Harry Fisher shirt, with its double-weight fine poplin and the collar's stitched edge, which gave it a firm shape. Harry sold the most beautiful silk ties, cut off the square as it was called and hand-made, naturally. He also sold those white stiff collars that I was rather partial to. So this became my sanctuary for a while and I didn't mind the long, achingly boring hours too much since there would always be a smattering of customers.

Unfortunately there is always a fly in the ointment: a dumb, fawning assistant who always liked to assert his snotty presence all over the place. This manifested itself at its most loathsomeness when I was serving an attractive female customer. He would actually barge into my sale as if indicating that I was incompetent when the reverse was certainly true. He just wanted to ogle!

Of course any degree of intelligence might make you aware that it is the grossest bad manners to step into a sale as if you were the important slug. Indeed, it made me seethe with rage. This inspired my 'writing' period and my relief was to set down all my hate and loathing for him in a journal. He had virtually no conversation apart from shop duties and I tried to avoid him as much as possible in that small room of the store, which as you can imagine was somewhat difficult. The boss, Harry Fisher, knew exactly what I was feeling and even sympathised with me. Fortunately I could seek relief at one of the lunchtime jive clubs that were springing up in the West End. The one I liked was the 51 Club, in Little Compton Street, W1, which played records between 12pm and 2pm. I would rush down there, which might take 10 minutes, dance for another 40 minutes and then rush back all sweaty, but what a divine relief it was and such fun!

One day when the vile manager was at lunch I actually vented my complaints to Harry, who confessed to me that he was completely sympathetic. He agreed his manager wasn't the brightest spark in the firmament but pleaded with me just to try and get on. So I stayed for about four months. It's curious how potent is just one single expression of kindness or affection. Once, when having his lunch downstairs (which was prepared by his wife), he even offered to share his cold borsht with me and I had never tasted anything so delicious and sometimes when slobbo wasn't there, he actually allowed me to examine the boxes of silk ties that the travelling salesmen brought in – long, fancy boxes. I remember how he would watch as I passed over some, picked others or deliberated. It must have been galling to the poor salesman to have this snotty 16-year-old judging his goods but it made me feel very proud and somewhat worthy.

So, the time passed but I felt that although Fisher was a high-class shop, it was a couple of rungs down from W. Bill and the little store was too small, really, for the three of us. I have a feeling that Harry might have been a boxer in his youth since he had a pugilist's flat nose and a boxer's stance. I really don't know what happened, but maybe he couldn't take the conflict between two of his staff and so one day he said it might be better if I moved on. I'd been there a long time by my standards and was not sorry to have a change. When I left, he wished me well and I could see he had tears in his eyes. Somehow I knew he really cared for me, maybe as a son, since I never heard him speak of having any kids. I never saw him again but I believed I loved him as a father, as a friend, an ally and I miss his lovely warm expression and soft brown eyes even as I write this. He was a man in a million.

Funnily enough, years later his dreary assistant opened his own shirt shop so the poor man was wedded to shirts and ties for his entire life. But good luck to him! He was probably good at heart and just couldn't stand me. It's a noble profession and an ancient one. So, to fill in the time I joined the YMCA for only £4 a year, played endless games of handball and read the want ads in the *Menswear Weekly*.

I started to drift again, unmoored, unattached, unstable, still obliged to meet the paternity payments. My relief was the YMCA and pounding the ball against the wall but the taxi drivers who came in the lunch hour were so good, you could scarcely score a point off them, no matter how hard you tried. When I did get a game I felt so relieved after. A good sweat and a hot shower, then a cup of tea and a sandwich was the most satisfaction I needed in a day. Without being too selective since I needed a weekly wage, I took a salesman job in a grotty second-rate menswear shop halfway down the Edgware Road, then a long twisting scar off Marble Arch.

I always had strange feelings about Edgware Road as if it did not quite belong to London – or if it did, it was an infected limb – and the shop in which I found myself was a great raw chancre in the centre. It was a low-class establishment selling mass-produced shit in the popular style that characterised the 1950s: pseudo-styled impersonation of Yankee fashion and fake camel-haired coats, fancy cheap sweaters and loads of suits in the grubby backroom. The vile Guv'nor sat at the rear like a great spider, sucking on a perpetual fag that stained his slimy moustache. He had a strange northern accent and was, as most retailers in the men's trade, Jewish.

171

His assistants seemed to be mostly misfits recruited from a Labour Exchange in hell, particularly one small greasy slob with a limp, who was always cracking sly, dirty jokes and an older man with almost white hair and a humble demeanour, who looked like his only recommendation was that he must have been cheap. The place was no joke but nobody interfered with my sales and I ate the lunch that Mum made in the stockroom upstairs and if very bored, had the occasional 'Levy and Frank' upstairs in the stockroom. Dirty! The Guv'nor called us by numbers so when a customer came in, he might say, 'Forward, number two... Forward, number three...' Then off you'd go. And he practised all sorts of seedy tricks, like badgering the customers when they were just looking in the window – 'Forward, number three!'...

However, I did make friends with such a cute little Hackney girl who worked in an equivalent ladies' shop down the road. A dyed blonde with short hair, she was sweet as a nut and I really enjoyed her cheeky, happy company. She was deeply affectionate and so responsive to my touch that she burst into bloom with the first rays of sunshine! Her family home was a happy one in the council flats in Hackney and she had a sister and brother and somehow they all looked alike. This passed quite a bit of time and at least I was on home ground again with a nice, wholesome girl. Quite frankly, I enjoyed her company and felt quite a few pangs for her but after a while the loathsome shop wore me down: the long journey from Manor House to Holborn, change and then Marble Arch and a packed tube-train only made bearable by the occasional frottage which sometimes came my way and then the long walk down Junkware Road.

The horror of that store and that street somehow infected my morale and I felt myself growing seedier and was visited by all sorts of vile temptations and strange offers by the odd assortment of low lives crawling down the street, but l stayed on my own path. I then decided to make the most of it and even tried to earn Mr Spider's respect. One day the filthy beast was taking a week's holiday and I decided to clean up the grubby storeroom in the back, so when he returned he would be amazed at my endeavour. It took me a whole week: first of all, I cleaned and polished all the gigantic mirrors in the huge backroom and then sorted all the suits into shades and sizes but the low scum could hardly bring himself to praise me when he returned so it was time to get out of that mausoleum.

Although I was paid on the Friday and could easily have failed to turn up on the last Saturday, to their surprise I did. At the end of the day the spider could only spew out from his dirty mouth the words, 'OK, you can blow.' The shop slowly died with its occupants in a ghastly slime and Edgware Road breathed a deep sigh of relief.

How I loved the summers! They were carefree times and when I was unemployed (not too often), I had not the slightest vestige of guilt as I took off to the Serpentine Pool in Hyde Park on a hot day. I'd get the Underground straight through to Knightsbridge and walk through the park. First, I would be greeted by Epstein's wonderfully energetic statue of the family and their dog racing into the park – that set my mood; then I'd walk through the tree-lined gravel paths delighting myself with the sights of happy people rollicking through the glorious summer days and of course I'd get there early before the crowds. Soon I'd be lying flat out with a book and taking the occasional baptisms. Sometimes my friend Barry Wise would come with me and we just had such a good time together but sometimes I went alone. But I never felt lonely since I had the park and the lake and the trees and sky and so the summer seemed endless. I'd spend as much time as possible there – if not working, it felt like the best and worthiest thing to do – and I'd keenly wait until the next summer when I'd return to the park and look forward to seeing the regular faces back again.

I'd now taken a job as a kind of warehouse boy in a textile house called Garigue in Golden Square as the lowest of the low, the person who cuts out with pinking shears little bits of cloth to make pattern bunches for the tailors, in and around Savile Row. It was on the top floor and there was a glass roof, which had everyone sweltering in the summer. So this is what I had to do, hour after pointless hour. In the shelves were beautiful end cuts of cloth, cut when the bolt was near its end, then it was sent upstairs to be used as samples and so we all sat there cutting patterns with our huge shears. Now I needed and craved a real suit, not one of Dad's botchy, ill-fitting numbers, grudgingly made and so one day I took one of the bolts of cloth scheduled to be shredded and it was actually enough to make a suit, three and a half yards. It was fine worsted with a strange, rusty colour and I took it to the current 'hot' tailors: Diamond Bros. on Shaftesbury Avenue (they made those elegant waisted, full-chested suits much favoured by the 'Blades' of Stamford Hill).

I climbed to their small workshop and fitting room, where I explained exactly what I wanted: a very stylish three-button suit with narrow legs. Diamond suggested having what he called 'French' cuffs on the pants (double-size turn-ups), to which I agreed most readily. I then went back for three fittings until it was done and it was perfect. I'd never seen anything *so beautiful* in my life – I was happy as a monkey and couldn't wait to wear it. Now I could go to The Lyceum with a bit of flair, or even the Whisky a Go-Go, the current favourite, which in our eyes was a real cool place now that the Cha-Cha had invaded our shores and there was another flaming dance to learn.

My daily work was deadly tedious but it gave me a weekly wage and I was, I suppose, learning a lot more about textiles,

175

though not much else. I'd have to wait for the weekend to go to the lido but since the management were fairly relaxed, I did skive the odd day off. As it so happens during one of my jaunts to the lido, I met a very nice, slightly older lady from New Zealand and had quite a bit of a flirt with her in the park, after which we got down and dirty but didn't go the whole hog. Strangely, although we had just met I formed a bit of an attachment to her. She was a real nice wholesome tawny New Zealand woman, about 10 years older than me, and of course in those days I never realised that I was highly toy-boy material. Eventually she took me back to her little room in Bayswater, where we went to bed but I was still never allowed the full Monty. Looking back, I believe she was actually a lesbian but had the occasional sweet spot for her lost youth.

Returning to work, I still had her scent on my hands and that comforted me for some days since I wouldn't wash it off – sometimes a woman's smell can be quite comforting after the event. She introduced me to Vernon, a fellow Kiwi in the same house, who lived in another small room on the ground floor. He had a soft smiling face and was gay. However, now I had two friends who were both cultivated, cultured and from a completely different world as it was possible to be. It was a world I liked since they were gentle, humorous and informative and that was pulling something out of me, something new, something that until then had no outlet and just sloshed about like a septic tank. Now I was learning stuff. So I started going out and meeting their friends and they would take me to the exotic coffee bars that were sprouting everywhere and introduce me to rather more interesting people than the ones I'd been used to.

Now one day Vernon suggested we go to see a play and this was something I really looked forward to. The first straight play I had ever seen, although I did take Ma to see a charity premiere of *Guys and Dolls*, which I found tediously old-fashioned. It was *The Rivals* by Sheridan and starred Laurence Harvey, then a young movie star. I enjoyed it, but I thought that what they were doing – walking around the stage without too much passion or effort – looked a bit easy. It was at the Garrick Theatre, whose stage I would occupy three and a half decades later.

I was a young, thin callow youth of 17. Oh, Vernon, if you could have only seen me in the future! Vernon Jones was his name. If he is still alive, he'd be an old chap but I hope he's still thriving somewhere in some backwater in New Zealand. Anyway, you took me to the Garrick and something opened in my head; something got planted there and I thank you, Vernon, for your help and patience and guidance. You helped pull me out of the morass with your intelligent chatter and your brilliant piano playing.

Oh, the summer was hot that year and the warehouse sweltering! I had a nice pal there, also simple and uneducated like myself, but we had a lot of fun just horsing around. He was a big strong guy and we chatted most of the day while we were doing our little cutting chores. One of those hot days, when we were all in a low, bored and frustrated mood, I accused him of taking my shears, which I had seen him using (blunt shears were a pain in the arse). He just looked at me then turned away, saying they were his. And so I asked him again and he looked up and just stared at me and I knew then that he had somehow lost it: he looked barmy. Before I knew what I was doing, I grabbed the shears which he demanded back, still looking wacko. It was then that I cracked him over the head with the handle. He didn't flinch or react: he just stood there for a second and then attacked me like a savage. Through the force of his onslaught, I fell to the floor and he continued by kicking me. Blood was everywhere and I didn't come out of it too well. Nobody interfered since it happened all too quickly.

I must have fallen on the shears since I had a deep cut on my wrist. I was rushed to the nearest hospital, which in those days was happily next-door. There my wrist was stitched up. I then returned to the warehouse only to be given my cards. I was sacked! Good fucking job, too. I'll go to the lido, I thought. But I liked that boy very much and I was sorry for what happened. I never saw him again but now in my memory I love him and hope he's well, with a happy loving family since he was such a sweet, gentle guy, really. I think his name was Norman.

Part IV

Leaving Home

Now it came to pass that 'information' circulated round the 'Hill' like Chinese whispers or Indian smoke signals. It began with my friendship with a nice kid called Wally, who could discuss ideas, books and how we saw our future. He told me that he had seen *Waiting for Godot*, which had just opened and that it had made a huge impression on him. He too was looking for some meaning in his life, like most of us brought up with a limited dip into the cultural pool.

We all wanted something into which to put our heart and souls so we seemed to share this combustible ball of energy bouncing around inside us like steel balls inside the pinball machines in the arcade on the 'Hill', living mostly on the end of our dicks, so thank God at least for that, that we have the most wonderful gift of love – except without some structure in our lives to sustain it, that too can very quickly decay. Well, Wally told me that a certain chain of retailers called Burberrys were opening outlets in PX stores all over Europe. Most, if not all American army bases, had these giant PX stores that supplied homesick US soldiers with all the junk they were missing from home. Also, the regular soldiers would have their families with them on the bases so the wives could keep up a semblance of family life, which was good for morale.

Burberry the famous traditional clothing store allowed their name to be used by a sub-contractor and these outlets, often manned by no more than three or four staff, were scattered all over Europe, even the Middle East and Iceland. The small outlets were situated at the corner of the PX store and carried only pattern bunches of cloth along with books containing all the available styles. Of course there were no fittings as the suits had to be made in Leeds or London and if they came back looking like a sack of potatoes they could always be altered by local tailors. This seemed like a great idea. Going abroad, what could possibly be more exciting?

So I went for the interview and shazam! I actually got the job. My menswear experience was pretty extensive and stood me in good stead so I was put on a training course at Ruislip army base. I just managed to pass muster but oh, the excitement of being on a base! It was the closest you could get to being in America. I knew how to measure a man for a suit and was careful always to have the metal end in my hand when measuring the crotch. After I got the job, I was sent by rail, boat and rail again to meet with the manager, a man called Collins, in Wiesbaden.

I left the country for the first time in my adult life and the thrill was overwhelming. It was a chill December when I arrived and made straight for the hotel, just across the road from the Wiesbaden Bahnhoff. I was now 18 and on my first big adventure in 1955, just 10 years since the end of one of the most horrendous wars in human history and of course, the Holocaust. I was astonished to find no blankets on my bed, just this huge fluffy duvet, but it kept me warm. I met Collins and he seemed pleasant enough, if a bit over-sure of himself. We had dinner together and discussed where I would be stationed, which was in a small town called Bitberg, about a day's drive from Wiesbaden. In the morning I explored my surroundings and it all seemed very weird and strangely fascinating, but now we were driving to my new home in Bitberg, a godforsaken town in the middle of nowhere, chiefly famous for its beer.

Our journey gave me a good impression of post-war Germany and we stopped off at a small hotel in Luxembourg for the night. After dinner we visited a bar for a beer and within minutes, were accompanied by two ladies grabbing our tools over our pants under the table and suggesting we go with them. All very exciting, of course we were too tired or rather far too nervous to take up the offer, just a bit of teasing on our part. Then we arrived in Bitberg. The company found me a room and board with a very typical German couple, who seemed quite pleasant. I had left home! I was happy, free, liberated and starving for adventure and here it was, I was living it. Next morning I met the two other guys running the place and they seemed most pleasant and young. They showed me the ropes and what was really exciting was that I could use the canteen and eat real Yankee burgers and re-taste all that I had so badly missed since I was 10 years old in New York.

The place was full of young Yankee soldiers, eager to chat about London and make friends – it was a gas from morning till night. They had a superb library and so I could really want for nothing except some female company but that was much harder to achieve since there were mainly soldiers and their wives on the base.

I was also earning a fortune since my wages were now a princely £18 per week, no small sum in those days so suddenly I was comparatively wealthy. Now according to my trained eyes, these Burberry suits were a pure scam. The only thing that was Burberry was the label: the suits came back looking like shit and nearly always had to be altered by a local tailor. The young soldiers had been shafted into thinking they had bought a piece of ancient British tailoring, with all the workmanship that the Burberry name stood for, but the suits had probably been thrown together by some cut-price sweatshop in Leeds. Nevertheless the soldiers didn't know zilch and there were few complaints.

Sometimes the salesmen, who were both Londoners and both Jews, brought me along for a night on the town with some of their US buddies but mostly I was left to my own devices. I was used to being alone and so I soon fell into bad old habits of courting my own company and found a pleasant little *konditorei* (coffee house), where I could sit in the evening with my journal, a glass of wine and a cigarette and sometimes that was better than listening to yuk yuk. However, there was a charming young German woman called Hanalore, a saleslady in the PX store, whom I managed to chat up. She told me she had a young child. We went out a few times but for no more than cuddles and a bit of desperate pressing.

The base had a movie house and a well-stocked library; they had all the kinds of books we never saw at my local branch in Manor House including some bizarre works of American fiction, which were quite astounding. But I chiefly liked sitting in my fave café and writing my diary. This was the beginning of my writing period, you might say. I seldom drank except for the occasional glass of wine but would mostly enjoy a coffee and the delicious German cake. So I was quite content and could not be happier exploring all the facilities on the base and finding many young friends since the US soldiers were always up for a chat. I was still blissfully content but then Christmas came and we were given three days off. This was my season in hell. My nice colleagues had all made plans that definitely excluded me and I was left alone. Very alone.

Today I have to ask myself what kind of humans these two characters were, not to ask if I would be all right, even invite me to join them for one of the days. For some reason, I always seem to be left alone at the worst times like Christmas. I hung about the house, had some lunch with my landlord and his wife and never knew such loneliness. It was horrible and so I returned to the store in an embittered mood. The following day I was briefly chatting to Hanalore on the floor before going for a break when a real brutish, Nazi-looking floor manager started shouting at her in German. So I shouted back at him and gave him some of my choice filthy-Brit curses. For that I was deemed a bad influence in the PX store and within a few days transferred to the beautiful city of Wiesbaden, where I would be much better off. Oh bliss! A tearful farewell to Hanalore, a train to Wiesbaden and a snug, really old-fashioned hotel room and all was well again.

Wiesbaden is a very pretty town divided by a large park down the centre with a fascinating network of streets to explore. I started to take an interest in the kind of German trinkets I never saw in London and bought myself a beautiful tortoiseshell lighter. The chaps in Wiesbaden were much friendlier and I was far less lonely for they were glad to have me around on our jaunts round the town. Of course high on the agenda was a visit to the Speilhaus, the gambling casino where Dostoyevsky lost all his money, just a century before. I never saw such a place in all my life: it was exotic beyond my wildest dreams. Groups of elegantly dressed players sat or stood round the tables, smoking. You could order cigarettes, which would be brought to you with the wrapping pulled back and a couple of cigarettes jutting out ready for you to pluck! Or order coffee or brandy while you siphoned your cash into the stomach of the casino.

A very heady place for a young man of 18! Very gingerly, I would place a modest two-mark chip on the red or the black, then flee, win or lose. The excitement was all too much and the thought of losing what I had worked so hard for, endured so much loneliness for, would be unimaginable.

I was saving zealously my money and had now amassed a small fortune of over £100, a couple of thousand today and a lot of dosh for me. I liked my real old cankered hotel too. At night they would serve supper and my favourite was oxtail soup or noodles with stew and a delicious salad served with the piquant German dressing. I even discovered a charming café/dance in Wilhelmstrasse and there I asked a lovely woman to dance. Her name was Fay and she was quite beautiful, with very dark hair, severely pulled back, dark brown eyes and a pale face with flawless skin. She became my regular date. On our first rendezvous she took me out in her large American car. She told me that she was married to an American officer. However, soon we made love on the back seat and nothing in the world was a sweet as that. I was in paradise!

It was really quite lovely, having such a nice girlfriend who was about 30 and I think I fell in love with her almost immediately. We had to be a little careful but she seemed to have a lot of free time. She'd take me to dinner or to nice little clubs where they had cabaret, a delight we seldom see anymore. And we'd always have such good time and she'd always insist on paying since I was her toyboy. She was simply adorable and ravishing. It was the most wonderful adventure yet and she seemed to take a great interest in me.

I confessed to her all my dreams and ambitions; how I wanted to reach far beyond what I had done with my life so far somehow, either as an actor or as a writer and once entertained fantasies of wanting to have piano lessons. She even offered to rent one for me! So the weeks passed pleasantly and peacefully enough and I was at last learning something – and that was German. Fay was German and seemed to be quite well off, so I had few qualms about being treated and it was most delicious to be spoilt. As all good things come to an end, it was decided by whatever the powers that be to get rid of the lazy bums manning the Wiesbaden branch of Burberrys and we were all given our notice. Now at such stressful times of change, how the Devil finds opportunities to slip in the cracks.

For some weeks I had been visiting the casino at least three times a week and had evolved a simple system which worked very effectively of putting two marks on red or black only when either colour had come up at least three times and if the colour came up four times, doubling up since I saw it was very rare indeed for one colour to come up more than six consecutive times. So, 2-4-8 and 14 marks would be the most I would be prepared to lose. Being cautious, I won most nights with my conservative method. And I loved the atmosphere of the casino and would always dress smartly since the dress code was de rigueur. I sat down and enjoyed it and after I had won £5 or £6, I was off. On frequent visits I never failed to chat to a very amiable man at the desk, who would always enquire in perfect English how I was. I would see this man at some future date – in fact, I would be working for him! One night I was a little more careless than usual and bet a slightly larger amount.

I waited for red or black to come up just twice instead of my usual three times and bet on the opposite colour. I put five marks on the black. Now it does occur every so often that an anomaly happens and of course this was the time. The red came up as if no other colour existed on the board and so 5, 10, 20, 40, 80, 160. *Ow, don't do it, don't do it, idiot!* But I had to recoup my huge loss and so 320 marks on the black and it was red. Red came up! Nine consecutive times, it was a record. A nervous wreck, I almost crawled away from the table: all my savings, all my hard thankless graft, four months living in dingy rooms. The horror of Bitburg and the vile work sweetened only by Fay and now it was all gone, all gone through my utter stupidity and greed. As I left the table I felt the eyes of the other punters all looking at me with pity, compassion even and this filled me with even greater shame.

I had met a highly intelligent young girl, a student called Edith, with whom I became friendly in a non-physical way and I went straight to her house for consolation. She sat with me, comforting me as if I was a victim of shellshock. Edith made coffee and we listened to the radio till dawn, then I went to my hotel and wept my head off. The next day, which was to be my last, I reported in sick since I just couldn't face it anymore; I had had enough. My return tickets were given and all the chaps were due to take the midnight train from Wiesbaden to the coast (Ostend, I think) and then the boat to Newhaven. That evening, Fay and I went to our usual café/dance, talked about the future and I resolved to come back.

I was coming back anyway since I had discovered a plastic surgeon with a clinic just opposite the Eagle Club, the American service club that I used to visit and where I even took piano lessons. I had asked the teacher if she knew of this surgeon and she promised that she would find out what she could. When next I came for a lesson she said she had heard he was first rate. I didn't like the little bubble at the end of my nose that I had inherited from my darling mother and if I was to be a movie star one day, I would have to have it dealt with.

So yes, darling Fay, I would be coming back. She drove me to the station to catch the midnight train. I didn't expect what happened next: I simply broke down. I broke down in a way I had never broken down before. Not just cried, but howled and howled – l howled like a child, l howled like the world had come to an end, howled like I had found the love of my life and lost her. It was terrible. I hugged her and we both wept like it was a flash flood: so terrible, so intense. There was a terrible weakness in me, a wound deep inside me that could only be fulfilled by a woman like Fay. And then I got out of the car. The guys were waiting by the ticket office. Then we got on the train and for some reason I immediately felt better and we played cards for the rest of the journey. Soon I was home again.

Being in love is the best buzz in the world. Maybe this was the first time that I had really experienced the power of it: how every frustration you have ever had, every disappointment, actually becomes fuel for it; how it wipes all pettiness of the world away and you only live for the object of your love. And if by some chance it is torn away from you, the rage within you gets stirred: the pain, the disbelief and the poor starved beast within howls; howls with a cry of pain that shocks you to your core.

Being home was good, too: to be in my own room again, to be looked after by Ma. By now, Dad had his own small tailor's shop in Brixton and I just have to admire him for starting up again in middle age, quite an achievement even if I only went there once or twice. I was never encouraged to visit. He still stayed out on Saturday nights to go to the 'baths' and on Sunday mornings brought home his usual guilt offering of a big bag of fruit. Of course this would provide a handy distraction for the awkwardness of coming in around 11am, all innocent. Obviously he had a mistress and it must have been going on a very long time – who knows, I might even have a half-sibling!

He was getting quite a reputation in the area for making suits exclusively for black people, or shall we say Caribbeans and catered exclusively to their style, specialising in what they called the zoot suit. We rarely had any visitors any more. He actually brought a young blonde lady to visit, who he said was an occasional helper in the shop and wanted her to meet his 'actor' son. I suspected his relationship was a tad warmer than just the occasional help. Maybe he even brought her home as a kind of peace offering to me and I wasn't inclined to reject his noble gesture. However, after 'abroad' London did feel deadly dull and unexciting. I missed my ambulatory life and of course, my lover Fay. I wrote a long passionate letter to her and she wrote a long passionate letter back and then I responded with another equally passionate letter as did she, then suddenly it all stopped as if we just spent ourselves out. (I still have her letters and how they become even more poignant with time.)

But now I had met an absolutely beautiful French girl called Jacqueline, with whom I fell intensely in love like a ton of bricks. We only went to movies and explored with each other's nice parts in the dark and under my coat lain across our laps. She had a simply gorgeous body and was dying to get into bed but since I was living at home and in those days children did not shag their loved ones under the same roof as their parents but in back alleys or parks, you mostly had to make do with a hard squeeze and a rub against a wall. She, my darling one, was getting fed up with that and who could blame her?

I had to get my own space, that was imperative but I couldn't see how on my small and irregular wages, so we continued cuddling and fiddling in darkened cinemas. Meanwhile, I was longing to get back to Germany but with little success since there was only one other firm sending young men out to the bases and that was Smart and Weston, a modern low-grade tailoring chain with a main branch in Oxford Street and so they sent me there until a post came up.

Working in a menswear shop can be extremely depressing since the hours are long and being on your feet all day is exhausting. Most of all, in my case anyhow, it also brings a distressing sense of worthlessness. And so the hours go by, it feels as if your life is just trickling out of you and that brings with it a sense of shame. However, they weren't a bad bunch of guys there and I befriended a charming Polish guy, who was extremely attractive in a rugged sort of way, had lots of girlfriends and came to work in an open-top Ford sports car, which he parked right outside the shop (which you could do in those days). The manager, as usual with managers trying to prove their worth, was a small, runty guy, who liked giving me chores such as handing me a broom and saying 'Give the floor a bit of a lick, Steve,' a humiliating job which for obvious reasons I hated (I was a tad over-sensitive in those days about what tasks I was assigned). The weeks sped by, my young life swept day by day into the dustbin and then lo and behold, I was offered a job in the PX store in Iceland, the dead end for PX stores.

Germany seemed to be drifting further and further away and though I asked about Germany or France, they fobbed me off, saying nothing was coming up for some time and they had guys on the waiting list for those places so it was a take it or scum it around Oxford Street, for God knows how long. I have no doubt the manager gave a lukewarm report on my talents and so I was sent to the worst place on earth, where no one but misfits went. So, one day I bloody went. I had to fly from Glasgow. Fortunately it was summer and when I arrived at midnight, it was still quite light in an eerie way. I arrived, wearing a smart black-and-white

Donegal tweed suit and a sweater, with my hair cut short. Since I saw no one waiting for me, I thought I would sit in the café and have a coffee and a fag.

The idiot manager who came to pick me up was probably looking for some dim geek, a reflection of himself. Eventually I spied this little man with glasses and staring eyes and introduced myself. He gave me a lukewarm welcome and showed me to my room, this time on base. Would you believe, I was sharing it with another twerp! So this was the pits, the worst location for all the losers and hopeless dummies. Accommodation was tight, he said, just share for a short time. So I ended up on the worst base while everybody was going to France, Italy, North Africa and I ended up in Palookaville.

The next day the manager took me into Reykjavik to get registered and then drove me to the little shack for Smart and Weston crap clothing. It was a dead awful place in a corrugated hut and the staff out of *Cuckoo's Nest*, poor things. I was determined to leave as soon as possible but in my usual manner I explored the base and made friends with all sorts of people – mostly young soldiers my own age, with whom I would have endless chats. I loved to visit the canteen since the food was remarkably good, the steaks unbelievable. I'd chat to anyone and soon had mates since Americans are so open and easy to befriend. I even made a friend who turned out to be gay but he liked my company and didn't press his sexual interests on me since he just liked talking to me so much about life in London, which I, of course, romanticised ridiculously.

There were lots of guys there and of course few women, being such an outlandish place, so a lot of guys might have sought some sexual company from each other out of sheer desperation. No big deal. One day a couple of academics who were teaching on the base got into conversation with me about the theatre, which I still felt was to be my eventual goal. They asked me to take lunch with them, which of course I did and we were having such a pleasant time that I didn't realise I had to be in the scum hole shop, so one of the teachers said: 'I'll just call and say you won't be long, and that *you're in a meeting!*' Well, this almost drove the manager gremlin into a fit. From then on, my time was marked and the freaks in the shop were looking for any way to get rid of me.

The weeks peeled off my life with dreary days and slightly better nights, the odd dance at the local hop and visits to the hot springs with my new pals. I even had driving lessons and odd piano lesson too but there were the long nights with their incessant twilight and the rest was incredibly dull. No wonder only the 'Z' group got out here, including me! However, with my usual inventiveness I became a small entrepreneur since I was allowed a liquor allowance from the base of two bottles of spirits per week at a real low tax-free price. Since I hardly drank in those days, I sold them on to the taxi drivers, who would pay an enormous amount for such treasures since the economy in Iceland was quite insane and I started to save again for my future trip to Germany.

Eventually, one of the vile and loathsome group with whom I had so unfortunately found myself informed on me to the boss that I was doing this (it was quite illegal). Not only this but the misfit actually read my diary, which was full of exotic thoughts and my disparaging opinions about them and had all the evidence they needed to swiftly put me on a plane to Leeds. None could have been happier than me. The twisted shrimp of a manager even wrote out a filthy letter that I was to give them to get my wages in lieu of notice. Well, I soon steamed that open and to say it was the most disgusting tome I had ever read would be an understatement, but apparently I couldn't get my wages without delivering the letter so I took a deep breath and delivered. The manager read it in front of me without so much change of expression, gave me my wages and I went happily home.

Whatever happened to that small bunch of sad wilted men I would never know but I knew life was becoming progressively more difficult and that I would never fit in with that kind of work. Ever. I needed to be with people who fulfilled me and still I had nothing, had learned nothing and was nothing more than a bunch of needs: just needs and vacuous dreams. Where to go, what to do? And the vague and distant fantasy of being an actor. The summer came and went, as did the odd pointless jobs I took on just for wages at the end of the week. Nights were spent hanging about or going up West, where there were lots of jazz clubs – The Flamingo, the '51' on a Sunday afternoon, The Lyceum on Sunday night and 'the women come and go'. Slowly but surely, I was drowning in a morass of pointlessness.

I was back in Manor House, back in my little bedroom. My anchor, my rock, my stability was my mother who was always steadily there for me, always: my breakfast always ready, my thoughts expressed and listened to, frustrations absorbed and calmed, dreams encouraged, hopes encouraged. Ma, believe it or not, would walk all the way to Stamford Hill just to save a couple of pennies on the bus fare. She'd get the tasty delights that she knew I loved and lay them all out for me and when I brought a girlfriend home, though rarely, she would purr and fuss over her and make her feel so welcome. If my current girl was a French au pair, as many were, Ma would make the girl feel so much at home and I would feel better and more positive since I could show them that I had a normal home and a normal mother. And there would always be a nice dinner on the table at night waiting for me.

And I watched Ma slowly growing old, so slowly but gradually old and sadly unfulfilled by her brutish husband, who never took her away on holiday but went 'alone'. Somehow she filled in her time doing the *Daily Mirror* crossword in the morning after breakfast and in the afternoon playing bingo in the local bingo hall, so very proud when she won a few bob. In the summer she liked to go and sit in Finsbury Park with the other old birds. Since Dad never took her away, she would book one of those Thomas Cook holidays and she knew there would always be someone who talked to her, a couple who would take pity on a solitary middle-aged lady yet find her charming and friendly, with a good sense of humour and keep enjoying her company. So she got used to going away each year by herself to the most exotic places and sending a postcard saying how much she enjoyed it. Sometimes Aunty Betty and Uncle Sam would come from the East End and for a few hours the place was full of noise and laughter and then it was quiet again. One day at my insistence we went out and bought a record player and some records and we mightily enjoyed that. That was another first in our lives. There was always a bottle of sherry on the shelf brought back from some Spanish trip but only rarely dipped into. It was just there in case we had company and a reminder, a souvenir, of happy times.

There were some photos of me on the mantelpiece and one of my sister, who was now happily married and living in some distant suburb. I clearly remember Beryl's wedding when she was 19 (I was just 12). Dad hired the cheapest caterers and even then baited them down. The food was appalling and everyone at our table tried not to complain, but in the end they had to give vent. Deeply embarrassed, I sat there. I remember Uncle Henry, Dad's brother-in-law, trying to placate the table by saying, 'Al has paid dearly for this', putting the blame solely on the low-life caterers, who were probably given the smallest budget to work with. My sister's husband Fred wasn't a bad guy and I actually got on well with him. One day he taught me how to print pictures and even bought me an enlarger. This was a revelation. It took some time to learn how to print but I persevered and at last I learned something! I spent hours with my chemicals and little prints.

So, thank you Fred, thank you so much. This time I persevered, since usually I come to a point when the going gets a bit hard and I give up the bloody thing, but here I persisted until all the clues fell into place. And so I took everybody's picture. Sometimes Ma would go down the East End to visit her sisters-in-law, Aunty Betty or Aunty Mary and that would pass the time. Poor Betty was a large, striking woman – not fat, but with a rather loud voice which she seemed unaware of. When they got on a bus together to go up West, Betty would embarrass Ma since the whole bus could hear her 'chatter'. But Betty was a nice aunt and never failed to make me welcome when I dropped by to see her and my beloved Uncle Sam in Cannon Street Road, E1. Sam never stopped talking since he had lots to say and most of it fascinating since he had had a lot of adventures. He was a compendium of everything he ever heard or read, or did and he lived in the East End all his long life. Even after he went blind in his sixties he would still walk miles every day. When I was a kid in the East End, he would always thrust shillings in my hand, though he was poor as a church mouse himself.

He wrote plays and books, though never had them published but he was honoured on that wonderful Cable Street mural of the local resistance to the fascist march in 1936 (his face is one of the young Jewish fighters). He has a son called Barry, who was quite bright and naturally went to university and studied dentistry, became an authority on the subject and gives lectures round the world. Uncle Sam was kindly, inquisitive, a natural father. One of the treats he had in store for us was a weekly jaunt to the West End on Saturday mornings to see the cartoons at the Cameo in Windmill Street but then again, I could be a pal to Barry, who was his only child. We'd take the No. 15 bus, get off at Piccadilly and spend an hour in the cinema then we'd walk all the way back along the Embankment! It was wonderful.

Barry got married to Sylvia and it was a nice wedding. I remember how well he conducted himself and made such a fine *mensch*-like speech; also thinking this will never happen to me – when I could be a *mensch* and stand with my beloved beautiful Jewish lady in a synagogue since I felt that this had already been crushed out of me. I don't know why but maybe because Shirley, my beloved from childhood, would have been the girl I would want to marry and since that had been thwarted, my hopeful ambitions in that direction were somewhat curdled. Barry predictably produced two fine children, one a homeopathic doctor and a clever daughter, who I believe became a lawyer.

Shortly after the débâcle in Iceland the next big thing going round the 'Hill' was to join the Merchant Navy. There were a certain amount of escape routes for us semi-educated slobs who lived for adventure since there was little else to live for and this was one of them. Since my dear father had zero interest in teaching me the magic craft of tailoring or helping him in his tiny shop, I drifted into whateverland with the others. My good friend Barry Wise told me of adventure and romance on the high seas but true to my form for bad luck, I got myself recruited onto *The Chusan*, a Mediterranean cruise ship for P&O lines, as a waiter in Third Class. I had my sister fake up some references since she was working for a large hotel company. She wrote that I had done silver service in first-class hotels and so off I went to Southampton, paid for my uniform and got on board.

To call this trip a nightmare would be an understatement. From morning till night, the work was hell since I picked a bummer: a holiday cruise ship with two sittings at every breakfast, lunch, dinner and the occasional tea. I was a hopeless waiter, completely and utterly useless, since I had never taken food orders before and was expected to retain them all in my head. Although I had two tables nearest the kitchen plus a dumb waiter, our table was always last to finish. And then you were rushed off your feet to prepare the table and clean your area in time for the next sitting. After breakfast I returned to the cabin, shared with at least five other seamen. But then it was lunch and that was a true nightmare since there were endless dishes and again my tables were the last to leave. But I have to say the customers were really patient with me and kindly; they even found me somewhat amusing and by the second week I was just getting used to it. A waiter's life on a cruise ship is a tough one and never will I underestimate their grit and courage.

Every other day when we were in a port I was allowed an afternoon off. It was simply fantastic to dock in Barcelona and since it was early morning there was a glorious yellow haze over the docks leading to Las Ramblas, that great avenue that goes to the centre of the city. It was such a beautiful shimmering dawn and I had never seen anything like it – this is what I thought 'abroad' means. All the passengers took off to see the wonderful sights, so lunch was cancelled or reduced for the few who stayed and I was set free. Eureka! I walked up Las Ramblas, sniffed around the side streets and had stepped into a small store to buy some fruit when I saw this rather luscious woman in a figure-hugging skirt giving me the eye. She invited me to go with her, which of course for me was nigh on impossible to resist. She was horribly sexy and we got on the bed and I feasted on her warm voluptuous body like a starving cat. It was such sweet relief, really heavenly, and as I was lying there I suddenly felt like a second course, to which she sweetly responded as if I was a naughty boy. I paid the fairly modest sum and wobbled happily back to the ship.

After my adventure we circled southern Spain and dropped anchor at Cannes. This time the ship stayed out at sea as the harbour was not large enough to take it and we were ferried in and out. The day was overcast and I found the beach strangely narrow. At night after we had served dinner a few of us went ashore and strolled happily free for a few blissful hours. We found a cheap café at the end of town and enjoyed our simple fare of tasty steak and chips. As we looked out into the night and saw that great liner lit up like a Christmas tree, we couldn't help but admire the sight and agree with the one joker among us who said: 'Look how beautiful it is! Who would think the ship is the bowels of hell?'

A merchant ship attracts all sorts since it basically needs raw labour and every scumbag and riff-raff would gravitate to it, not so differently to the old whaling ships of the past. There were lots of drop-outs, ex-university types who lost their way, failed businessmen, losers and criminals but they usually worked in the kitchens and laundry and cleaning, while we waiters were meant to be just one step up. We dropped anchor at Naples and that was a treat to see the bay of Naples and the great Vesuvius thrusting itself into the warm Neapolitan air.

All this was a great adventure, unfortunately soured by the horror of the work we were doing. On my few hours off, as I was strolling in my usual aimless fashion I came across some street urchins, who inveigled me into going inside a restaurant and buying them a pizza. I didn't mind at all since I was glad of their company, even when they giggled their heads off, as if so delighted with what an easy dope I was and how smart they were to blag a meal out of me. But I quite liked being taken for a fool since I found them such delightful company. When I paid and we all got outside the smallest one of the group, the least corrupted, obviously felt a pang of guilt and he came up to me with a slice of melon he had just bought from a street vendor. I was so touched by that little urchin handing me the melon that the memory has always stayed with me.

But now we were on our way back and it was too warm to sleep in the crowded cabin so I took a blanket and slept under a canopy of stars and it was wonderful. After a couple of days we docked at Southampton and by then I had frankly had enough, so I quit and spent the rest of the day sitting on deck until we were released. Thank you, Merchant Navy and goodbye! I wasn't quite up to your rigorous demands; also it turned out, I wasn't well. So back to Manor House and Quo Vadis.

I believe the stress of my teenage years had provoked an outburst of duodenal ulcers, which periodically caused me a great deal of pain and so I checked into a local hospital for treatment, which in those far-off days was to slide a milk drip inside your nose to your stomach and just live off that for more or less a whole month. But that was one huge bore and soon after I left the hospital, it returned again. My darling mum visited me, bringing cigarettes, which unbelievably you could puff in your bed in those ancient times. Who would believe the time would come when antibiotics would get rid of it? I still craved to get back to my beloved in Wiesbaden and it was almost becoming a biblical quest; I felt I was being sorely tested and shunted about, just flopping on top of a giant wave, being deposited willy-nilly wherever it wished. Just living, surviving, adventuring, loving and in between somehow cast into a most dreadful limbo, a nothingness inside my council flat in Manor House. And in the end knowing nothing, learning nothing and still achieving nothing.

I felt that it was about time to make my own decisions, to attempt to guide myself without being dragged in the slipstream of whatever meaningless occupation I could attach myself to and so I decided to go back to Wiesbaden under my own steam. Now I had a dual purpose: not only to see my darling Fay after 18 months but to get my nose done by the plastic surgeon I had seen the last time I was there. I wrote to him and he replied promptly, giving me the cost and even booking me in. As usual, darling Ma helped out and loaned me £50 just to get going, so one morning I set off on the channel ferry to Le Havre and then the train to Wiesbaden.

When I arrived I went straight to the youth hostel for the night, but my mind was full of misgivings: 'Oh, full of scorpions is my mind, dear wife…' I had breakfast with a fellow lodger, a student hiking through Germany and I told him of my plight. He was such a pleasant and sensitive soul and when I talked to him about my quest and my fears and whether to do it or not, he said that since this had been a dream of mine for so many years, I should do it. 'Take the risk, it will be OK,' he assured me. Oh, what a decent and sympathetic young man. So that morning I turned up at the clinic and once again met the elegant, silver-haired surgeon, who was most suave and smoked with a long cigarette holder. He showed me a book of all kinds of noses and I said I just wanted it slightly slimmer and to get rid of that bulbous bit on the end which characterises my entire family of aunts and uncles but would end, please God, with me. 'More like a "French" nose,' I said, thinking of those strong, straight noses I had seen in French movies. 'OK,' he said, 'please go into your room and take off your sweater and vest, and get ready.' He was prepared to start immediately!!

One thing disturbed me above all and that was whether to keep my Star of David round my neck. My mother had given it to me but naturally it would be impossible for the thought not to cross my mind that, given his background, he might be tempted to mutilate me. So I took the risk, and kept it on and prayed. He gave me a few injections to numb the nose area and before I knew it or even suspected, he smashed an instrument down upon my nose. Bang, bang! He was breaking it first in order to reshape it. For a while, I heard him scraping away and this seemed to go on for some time; I felt nothing but only heard the scraping. Then the anaesthetic seemed to be wearing off and I was feeling pain, but finally it was over. He plastered over my recon-structed nose to keep it in place and I was put to bed.

The next day I awoke with a pair of black eyes but I felt relieved, so relieved and happy. I searched the paper under the heading of 'Zimmer' (rooms) and was able to talk in English to a very nice, cultivated woman who had a room in Grillparzer Strasse, which was not far away. I went round and I met this woman, a Fraulein Schmidt. It was a pleasant room in a charming house and I felt really lucky. At least I was doing things for myself and at 19, I was independent, living on my own in a foreign country and learning German. Hey, things were getting back on track!

I couldn't get around too much with my *Phantom of the Opera* mask, but I did see my sweetheart Fay. Unbelievably, something had died between us: she was warm but rather matter of fact, even slightly polite. I don't think she had any love for me anymore. Was it the operation? Did she think of me as some vain tosser when she loved me just as I was? After a few days it was time to get the plasters off and I could not believe it: I was transformed. My face felt new and for the first time, I really felt that I was handsome. I could start life again and fulfill my dreams of becoming an actor since my infantile mindset believed good looks were all important. Now there was nothing in the way that had to be my immediate goal, but in the meantime I was keen to find some paid work and somehow managed to get a job as a waiter serving drinks on an American base, which was really great fun but exhausting work, even if it was relatively easy: Americans are good to chat to and get along with – and they don't get aggressive when they're drunk. On payday the place would go berserk, the bar was packed and they'd leave large tips since these Yankees are generous spirits, no doubt about it.

I saw Fay a couple more times, but the spark had gone and I even saw another darker side to her, which I never ever suspected. It was such a shame but I didn't love her anymore either. It was during this visit when I was told that I could visit the American service club (The Eagle, I believe), a very pleasant place to drink and eat, where officers could take their wives. Lo and behold, there was the same man who was at the reception in the Speilhouse where I suffered my traumatic loss, 18 months earlier! Now a freelance rep for Rosenthal china, he was doing his spiel to a group of eager American ladies from a table where he displayed some of his wares. After the crowd dispersed, we chatted and he seemed pleased to see me again. In fact, he asked if I would like a job. He could use an assistant, he said, when he went touting round the bases and would pay expenses and food money.

Oh how kindly fate can treat you when you take the first step yourself into the uncertain world! I gladly accepted and so I began travelling with him. In the morning at about 9am I would walk to the flat where he lived with his ageing mother and we would eat a lovely breakfast together on the terrace, actually the basement: rolls and cheese and coffee, that delicious German coffee (not like the British muck) and then we would drive off. It was my greatest adventure yet.

Fritz Peil spoke perfect English and was utterly charming and very funny. Like few men I had ever known, he had wit and could use it to devastating effect. He had an endless fund of stories and loved to regale me with tales of his times in the Army. I could see he was certainly gay but it never interfered with our relationship and not once did he suggest otherwise. Looking back, I think it was more of a father-and-son relationship. For me, his selling technique was a wonder to behold. The American family housing unit was the target of our operations. He'd knock on the door and merely introduce himself as a Rosenthal rep, who had come only to show his beautiful china with no obligation whatsoever to buy, then he'd lay his wares on the carpet and tell the story of Rosenthal while enchanting the bored housewife, who would be suddenly taken out of her dull routine by the conjuring of a man and his 'handsome' young assistant. I watched in avid fascination and at least a quarter of the time the women would be persuaded to make an order then I would carefully put the china back in the cases. It was the greatest training I could ever have. After a couple of orders we would go for a light lunch and carry on in the afternoon. I was very happy to swing along as the sorcerer's apprentice.

Sometimes we would drive to outlying bases and then in the evening drop into Frankfurt. There, he would head to the gay bars while I would explore the straight bars and meet up in a couple of hours. I certainly felt like the character in Thomas Mann's beautiful novel, *The Confessions of Felix Krull, Confidence Trickster*. On the base I made friends and even had a young army couple to dinner that I had become pally with – the first time that I had ever entertained. I was free, liberated in mind and spirit and finding myself. The newly married pair took me to an amateur play put on by the services. I found it quite charming and again thought this didn't look too difficult to do. Up until then, I had only thought of acting as something you mainly do in movies.

The summer in Wiesbaden was hot and I went swimming in their nice open-air pool and noticed how everybody brought delicious picnics with them. But I was very much alone for apart from Fritz, I knew few people. I still enjoyed the work and had been there now for two months and was starting to think about moving on. I had met a French girl, Jeanine, a few months previously at the Astoria Dance Hall, Charing Cross Road, that rancid, but somewhat charming pick-up place for lonely au pairs, now just a memory. She had left London and was working in the South of France, at a place called Ax-les-Thermes in the Pyrenees. I promised her that I would visit and we had sent each other some letters. But then came a terrible stroke of bad luck, something that would stay with me for a long time, an act of madness... Oh, how I so easily undermine all my careful efforts!

It was a Sunday and I wasn't working. I was really bored and lonely, so decided to take the train to Frankfurt for a walkabout, which I did. Early evening, I got the train back. Well, it so happened that on the train I got into conversation with a rather sweet teenager who spoke very good English. She told me about all the things that she would like to do with her life and I told her of my adventures. When the train stopped at Wiesbaden, I invited her back for a further chat. Oddly enough, she accepted without hesitation. I knew she was young, maybe 16 or 17, but I myself was only 19. When we arrived, I attempted to demonstrate my affection with a cuddle when she suddenly froze and said she had to go. I realised that I had made a bad mistake since she was really naive and quite innocent. The next morning there was a knock on the door and I answered since Fraulein Schmidt, my landlady, was away for a few days and totally trusted me with her precious house. Until then I had shown myself to be completely trustworthy but the pangs of loneliness can turn us all into deviants and criminals. Well, two plainclothes coppers were at the door and questioned me. The girl was, in fact, jailbait and not much more than 14! Since the charge wasn't so serious as rape as I had only tried to hug her, I was told to turn up the next day in court. It was her youth that made the offence a little more serious and I was afraid they might put me in jail.

Following this, I decided to flee the town and packed my bags. I met up with Fritz, who was a bit surprised by my sudden departure, but still agreed to pay me some of my commission for a few of the jobs I did on my own. Now what was really stupid was to skedaddle off without leaving the month's rent for Fraulein Schmidt. I left a note saying that I would pay it later, hoping to appease her. Dumb fool I was turning into after such a promising start!

It was night: after a fond farewell with the only person who had ever really helped me in my life, my dear friend Fritz, I took the train to Perpignan. From there, I would take a train to Ax-les-Thermes. I had committed two crimes, both of which would come back to haunt me in the future since for some reason I am incapable of doing anything dodgy and getting away with it!

I had been momentarily thrown back into my old sleazy way of life, which made the path slippery with ordure. I had tried to make a new life – a new face, a fresh start, a good friend – and I had shat on everything. I was contemptible but sure I would wash myself clean… Please. The train journey to Perpignan took forever but on the last leg through France, I fell into conversation with an attractive young woman in her twenties and asked her if she might know of a cheap hotel in Perpignan. She replied that she was staying in a modest family hotel and I could try and get a room there. So we cabbed to the hotel and went to the reception, but the reply was that it was full. It was summer and all the hotels were busy. However, the receptionist said: 'But Madame, your room is a double, for two people!' So she said if I wished I could share the room, which I took to mean there were twin beds. But there was only one bed, one large double. Only in France could such an offer be made to a complete stranger to share a bed!

We had a pleasant and simple dinner together and I thought nothing of it since it was all done so innocently, so straightforwardly that any thoughts of nocturnal naughtiness were far from my mind. When we got to 'our' room, she even requested I wait outside while she undressed and got into bed. After a while I knocked and entered, then sat on the far side after brushing my teeth. I got undressed with my back to her and then climbed into bed. She switched off the light and I just lay there for a while. I was prepared just to go off to sleep but feeling a strange woman next to me put me in a state of high excitement so I couldn't even begin to feel drowsy. Slowly, very slowly, I let my left hand drift over to hers and held it. She didn't withdraw but held mine back. I was excited beyond anything I had ever known in my whole life. Slowly I turned on my left side and kissed her. She said: 'Dors, dors' (Sleep, sleep). Somewhat difficult, I would have thought, but then I found her mouth again, kissed her passionately and she responded. This went on all night long and while she wouldn't let me take any liberties with her beautiful gowned body, she allowed my own naked body to hold her tightly.

There is something extraordinarily delicious in being in bed with a complete stranger – you get to know each other sensually before you have the barest knowledge of each other's existence. Perhaps because it's forbidden, you haven't had to trade references before you are wrapped in each other's arms. It was ecstatic. I was so very happy again with this most lovely and charming French lady. And I do believe she was happy too.

The next day I took the train to Ax-les-Thermes, the beautiful little village high in the hills. Jeanine was so pleased to see me and I stayed in her small room at the hotel. We had a pleasant few days together but she was working most of the time except for the late afternoon when we would go up to the waterfall in the hills just above the hotel, where we would make love and then wash ourselves in the waterfall. Ah, what a life is youth and too swiftly is it gone!

The anxieties I suffered after the Weisbaden incident were slowly beginning to fade but I did wonder if I'd be in some kind of legal danger if I returned to Germany. I put it behind me as another one of those messes that I was prone to putting myself in.

After a few days my money was running out and it was time to go home. And so I did, this time stopping off briefly in Avignon. But then it was back to the horrors of Manor House. I had opened the door to other worlds, worlds of such possibilities and potential, but cravenly I crawled back to the familiar prison. Ma was waiting with dour news: Fraulein Schmidt had written to my mother! She wrote that I was a thief for not paying her the last month's rent; also, that I was wanted by the police for sexual assault. It was a foul note but it appeared to me that foul does seem to grow wings.

Fortunately my father never got wind of it since his method was always to condemn, accuse, berate, attack and never forgive, so the less he knew about anything the better for all of us. I felt soiled in front of my mother and did my best to appease her, inventing all sorts of excuses but felt it had now left an indelible stain. So all I could do now was to get a job, to get back on the treadmill until such time when I would wake up one morning and find myself turned into a gigantic actor! As yet I still didn't quite know where one went or what one did, so I would just have to fall into the old groove and get a job in another menswear shop. And so I did, and found myself in a very pleasant part of London called King's Road, Chelsea, working for a man called John Michael.

John Michael was a very pleasant young man who wore smart tailored suits and was set up in his shop by his mother (who owned the ladies' boutique next door). John (or 'Mr John', as he was so quaintly called) was a bit of a pacemaker in men's fashions in those so glorious days, which were just ready to burst into the 1960s – the signs were all there, it just needed a bit of a nudge. So, the shop was modern without being too bold, but bold enough for those who just wanted a nudge of innovation. It was on three floors –basement, ground and first – and this is where I lived, worked and trudged for over a year and I discovered the King's Road. Then it was a ragged kind of road, full of quaint coffee houses and antique shops, with a distinctly bohemian air so different to what it has sadly turned into. It was a long schlepp from Manor House to Sloane Square but I bought my monthly season ticket, which meant I could use it any time I wanted to, including nights and Sundays. In fact, my season ticket was my only sign of wealth since I didn't possess a bank account or a driving licence and there were no credit cards in those days.

To call this work numbing, tedious, boring, even soul-destroying would be the tip of the iceberg. However, it was a pleasant environment except for, as usual, the manager – an oafish old-school peasant, who thought he was in the Army and insisted on calling me by my surname. Lunch-times, I would go to a coffee bar across the road called SA Tortuga – unbelievably owned by the father of an actress called Linda Marlowe, with whom I was to work with in future years. I went to that café nearly every day and they made the most wonderful Liver Veneziana so even my tastebuds were becoming liberated. And of course they had one of these giant espresso machines that were springing up all over London as the city was became 'Italianised'.

John Michael was a gentle, friendly young man and always full of enthusiasm. On Saturdays, he gave his staff a commission on what they sold and so on that day the staff would go at it hell for leather. Sometimes I got to pop into the local antique shops and was ever so slightly impressed by the louche manner of the owners. How suave and cool were they, in their heavy black roll-neck sweaters and old leather jackets! Further up the road was a beautiful old building, The Pheasantry, then an elegant members club. I desperately needed to have a place where I could entertain my occasional girlfriend. For two guineas I was allowed to join and this was my second card of liberation. Further down the road was a small fashion boutique run by a charming couple who seemed to have pioneered the miniskirt, deeply shocking and exciting then – the shop was Mary Quant's first.

By now I had acquired my second Diamond Brothers suit, which was spectacular. A dogtooth black-and-white check, with full shoulders, double-breasted lapels and single-breasted do-up, it was dazzling. One day Quant's husband came into the shop, stared hard at me and said, 'What an amazing suit.' I was glowing with pride since I had more or less designed it myself. And so his praise was etched onto my mental notepad and never forgotten since it implied if nothing else at least I had boldness of taste. Just as lines of praise are seldom forgotten so malevolent ones are not forgotten either – and how many wicked lines I had to endure from my poor old dad. Unbelievably, quite a few from my competitive sister too, but then it was her 'humour'. But nasty lines are like acid: they have a way of etching themselves into your brain and staying there, like a tattoo, so I try to remind myself to say only good lines if I can.

At least in Chelsea there was a more exotic breed of fish to observe than I might have come across in some of the dreary dumps I had been working in. I was an obvious target for many who came sniffing round the shop, curious about the new guy on the block, especially if they were of the artistic bent – which is not meant to be a play on words and although a fair few were gay, it made absolutely no difference to me. As a young salesperson I would engage in all sorts of chat and if they were theatricals, my eagerness to know more seemed to draw a response from many of them.

I met a charming American called Richard Page, who had been studying at RADA and regaled me with stories about being a real drama student. He invited me to his very bijoux little house, in nearby Bywater Street. At that time, I was beginning to learn about actors, a completely new and fascinating breed who seemed mostly gay. I found that gay men liked to open up a conversation and even if the motive was at first perhaps sexual, once they had been made aware that your sexual predilections lay in quite another species of genital, a friendship often remained, as it did with Richard. I noticed his enthusiasm for musicals since gay people in the theatrical profession seemed to have an enduring passion for show business and dynamic bust-a-gut leading ladies and he played me an assortment of his shiny imported LPs, including the great New York hit, *West Side Story*. I was taking it all in and welcomed such input from him.

One day he demonstrated some acting. He acted out the 'gentleman caller' from *The Glass Menagerie* and I have never forgotten it – the way he went into it, how he almost threw himself into it. I was amazed at how an actor could not only transform himself but had the courage and audacity to just get up in front of a casual friend and perform. I was so taken by that performance I was determined to read the

play and play the part: it would be just up my street –
enthusiastic, brash, optimistic yet sensitive, concerned and
naive at the same time.

Another time a friend of his called Conrad Monk, also at
RADA, came round. He was a rather dashing young bloke,
quick to correct me in my speech and he instructed me to
be careful in the way that I said words ending with the
letter 'Y' and not to pronounce 'lonely' or 'body' as 'lonelee'
or 'bodee', but 'lonli' and 'bodi'. I was still sounding too
much like a London cockney. But I certainly made a note of
his instructions. Conrad was typical of the breed of
confident, well brought up, good-looking men who filled
the ranks of RADA at the time. He went on to do quite well
but then suddenly left the business and formed a company,
which became quite famous as 'Knobs and Knockers'!
Conrad sold a great variety of doorknobs and knockers in
every possible shape and size, apparently very successfully,
until he retired.

I stayed friendly with Richard, who one day invited me to
the performance of *Don Carlos*, directed by the great Visconti
and I was warned it would be a long haul. It was actually a
dress rehearsal and Richard, along with many other RADA
students, was playing an acting walk-on; he was responsible for two large beautiful dogs. It must have been during
a week's holiday that I had the time to go to Covent Garden
and sit through this interminable opera, which did indeed

seem to go on forever. About halfway through, I thought I'd pop into The Lyceum, conveniently situated just off The Strand and where they were still running lunchtime jazz sessions, where you could certainly purge your frustration for an hour, jiving to records. So I swiftly ran round to The Ly, had a few dances and then walked back to Covent Garden to resume my seat! They were still screeching away and sounding much the same as when I left, well over an hour before! Sadly they didn't have the sub-titles that make opera so compulsive today, so utterly enjoyable and comprehensible. Unless you are an aficionado without them it can be pure hell.

Sometimes Richard and I would go to a coffee bar in the King's Road, which was the 'in' place, where you'd sit at candle-lit tables, drinking wine and talking earnestly. It was there that I was introduced to a most charismatic black actor called Gordon Heath. I had never met anyone like him before in my entire life and of course it was only by being in Chelsea that I was given the chance to meet such remarkable people. Apparently he was a well-respected and reasonably famous actor who had played on Broadway. His voice was perfect velvet, fluent, elegant and most charming. It was in the same café where I came across the highly exotic, fabulous theatre hero Peter Wyngarde, who had the most elegantly beautiful voice I had ever heard – or at least comparable to my idols, Laurence Olivier and José Ferrer.

Those were rare times for me but I somehow took them for granted since they seemed to come with the King's Road territory. If only I had been just a tad more aware of the significance of these extraordinary people. However, I was aware of them enough to realise they were light years apart from what I had known.

Peter Wyngarde was just about to perform in *Duel of Angels* with Vivien Leigh and of course, this was something I was determined not to miss. So I went to see it and it was one of the most breathtaking performances I have ever seen on every level. Leigh was just immaculate, slender and beautiful beyond compare, with a low husky sensual voice, while Wyngarde was at the top of his form. He played at speed and yet with such a clarity as I had never before seen: he seemed to stand centre stage as if rooted like a tree and his voice streamed out into the universe at a colossal pace but with every sentiment clear as a bell. Now I saw what acting could be: I was mesmerised, spellbound, gob-smacked at every level. Wyngarde and Leigh on stage was a match made in heaven!

I gradually fell out of contact with Richard, which was a shame since he was such a friendly and gentle soul. Later, I heard he had become an agent. I of course followed Wyngarde's career with great and adoring interest, seeing him blast through our 12-inch black-and-white TV when he did *The Taming of the Shrew*. There was nothing like it. I was grateful to John Michael's as the shop sometimes became a kind of meeting place and it gave me the opportunity of meeting people I would never in my usual circumstances have had the chance of knowing. Once I met an eager young student who was studying at Central drama school and we engaged in some enthusiastic chat during which he told me of a fascinating tutor he had called Charles Marowitz. Lo and behold, one day he actually brought Marowitz in just to meet me! I found him to be quite engaging and have known him ever since.

The months were rolling past and I was getting to know quite a different type of human to my Neanderthal cousins around Manor House. Slowly, but surely I was pulling away from those old roots, even if in the future they would be a constant source of inspiration. Nothing will be wasted.

Apart from SA Tortuga there was a workman's café across the road, one of those relics of Victorian times, where you sat in booths with long tables. The booths had high backs and you were fed good, solid working-class British food – gourmet and cheap. What a shame these ancient treasures of London were torn out of our lives! Since we were in Chelsea it was not uncommon to have a well-known actor stroll in and one day I had the privilege of serving John Gielgud. Of course I served him with all the glutinous charm I could summon up, even asking him how the play he was in at the time was doing. He was the model of charm and decorum.

I was serving others, something I had done my whole life but I knew my time would soon come. Something would happen and something had to happen to make it all change, as it had when I went on my own to Germany. By changing my pattern, everything unlocked and I was free – but if you stick to a pattern then you gradually put the cuffs back on again!

Each morning as I left Sloane Square tube to walk down the King's Road to work at John Michael's I noticed there was a play on at the Royal Court Theatre called *Look Back in Anger*. I only recall it because I would see it each night as I walked back to the tube and one evening there was an excerpt on the black-and-white TV of a scene round an ironing board. Even to my untutored eyes it seemed rather wan and old-fashioned but I did notice a lot of bandying about of the term 'angry young man'.

Now not knowing where to start, I picked up *The Stage* newspaper and answered an ad for 'method' classes, this having been another one of those new-wave ideas from the cauldron of modern American theatre. There was a whole heap of scam studios sprouting up all over the place, attended by eager naive young idiots and of course I was one of them, entering the small Soho studio full of trepidation and awe, as well as envy of the bolder characters there. But it was through those classes at which I learnt nothing and gained nothing that I found out about *Spotlight*, the directory with the names of most people in the industry. Still not knowing what to do or where to go, I just wrote to as many film companies and TV producers as I could. Amazingly enough, most of them were courteous enough to write back and some suggested I go to a drama school, which to my simple mind seemed an awful waste of time and how on earth could I afford such a thing? But one person who I actually spoke to on the phone suggested that I start off by attending evening classes, to test myself so to speak and recommended I join up at the Holborn Literary Institute. So I went along for a brief interview and signed myself up for the drama course in the autumn term. This seemed a good idea for it meant that I could still work.

The Institute was conveniently situated in Stukeley Street, Covent Garden. One evening, I entered the classroom. It was full of young people, all pleasant-looking and friendly, alert, sensitive and all full of anticipation. So different from the Stamford Hill fraternity: the cuffs were beginning to loosen up, I could feel it. The teacher, a benign, silver-haired chap, began talking and my heart was thumping. I had taken the first step, even if it was only for two or three nights a week. He gave us an exercise to start with: he asked us to cross the room diagonally and described the movement as open and free, in abandon. So we did just that and then he asked us to do it again but this time to convey a closed, introverted movement – I believe the word he used was 'centripetal'. And so we all did that. I remember those moments so well, even if they were 50 years ago as I write. What a beautiful class and we were studying drama!

We'd do our exercises from 6.30pm until 8pm, then file into the canteen for coffee and return for another session. And afterwards we all, or at least some of us, would go to the coffee house in High Holborn and feverishly discuss theatre. Oh, *les beaux jours!*

I continued working at John Michael's, but gradually I was shifting out of the old zone and acquiring new friends. Now the talk was of plays, writers, actors and slowly I was beginning to see another world and making myself familiar with that world. Although I was given hints a few years back with Vernon from New Zealand, these were just isolated incidents, valuable and instructive, but now it was becoming a path. At last I was starting to see something being formed in front of me. I had made friends with a Canadian actor called Murray. He advised me to try and get into a drama school and study full time as this would get me into the business far more easily. There was one he knew of, a small school and not one of the famous ones, which might take me for the second year only, taking into account that I had spent some time at the City Lit in Holborn.

The City Lit had been and was still a home for me, where I was learning rapidly and with great enthusiasm. We were encouraged to get up and perform in front of the class, which I found very intimidating at first. And we were asked to choose a speech from a play, modern or classic. Well, I had never read a play in my life even though by now I had seen a few. All the plays that I read seemed to be broken up into little bits of dialogue and none too interesting at that, so I ransacked my collection of Kafka's short stories and came up with one that was like a little play. It was called *The Bucket Rider*, a charming little fantasy, or allegory, about lowliness and poverty in which a starving, but penniless man in need of coal decides to 'ride' to the coal dealer on his empty bucket. So I got down to learning it and it was about three pages long but it spoke to me far more than any of the plays I was trying to read.

No sooner had I began my tale than the teacher stopped me. 'No! No! No!' he ranted, 'That's not a play, you must find a play with a character!' Of course he meant well and was trying to guide me but I knew that I had found my métier: storytelling. One day I would perform Kafka's stories around the world, but for now I had to find a character and each week I did.

Although I now had some friends from the class, I still needed a mentor and for some reason I was always lucky in finding someone, usually an older man who would take me under his wing and help or guide me while finding my enthusiasm and need to learn fulfilling to them. So it so happened that a new person came to the classes as a kind of adviser or trainee teacher. Murray Gilmore was a highly cultivated and passionate Scot with dark brown luminous eyes and a most passionate way of speaking, which for some almost bordered on lunacy but I found him absolutely fascinating. I had never come across anyone like him in my life. And after each student got up and feebly did their chosen piece, he would almost jump up and tear them to pieces with such a stream of pure passion, excitement and rage it was a wonder to behold.

I was utterly fascinated by him and asked him to coach me from time to time, which he did and his training was absolutely invaluable. Alas, he is no longer with us. Eventually, he became one of my closest friends and mentors and I would visit him frequently at his flat, which was not far from me. We spent evenings in peals of laughter and he taught me much. Some nights, I even brought him home for supper and my mother also liked him enormously. The fact that he was a homosexual didn't matter a fig since I found many gays were, in fact, far more sympathetic to me than the straights and none made any attempt to woo me once they knew my predilections.

Murray at the time was in deep psychoanalysis, which may have led him to take up teaching at the City Lit, although he was a very fine classical actor even if he seldom worked. He often spoke of the old school of actors and directors with whom he trained, mentioning names like Tyrone Guthrie and John Blatchley, but I had never heard of them and only came across the great Tyrone Guthrie years later. After much soul-searching, I decided to try and get into a drama school, the one my actor friend Murray had recommended, the place that would be able to take me on for just one year. I thought I could at least hack that since I now knew that the only way into the business was through a full-time drama school. So I went to this small, quaint drama school called Webber Douglas, tucked away in Clareville Gardens just off the fashionable Gloucester Road, SW7. The comfortably padded Mr Rossiter listened to my two speeches, gave me sensible notes and said he could take me on, but I would have to find the money for the three terms and of course I had none. He advised me to write to the Arts Council for a bursary – which I did and was granted an audition at County Hall.

I received the application form which I had to fill in and found it not only daunting but also hopeless since it asked for details like how many 'A' levels I had, what degrees, what diplomas, etc., etc. I knew this would be my undoing for there was nothing that I could say. Nothing. So I decided to write them a letter and tell them the whole unvarnished truth. I told them about my broken schooling and how I left at the age of 15 without sitting any exams and that in the bleak years since then I had had nearly 100 jobs (believe it or not). Also, that I had learned nothing at my appalling school and all the jobs I had had taught me not one single solitary thing; that I was sent to a detention centre when I was 15 and had not found anything of any use until I discovered drama and since I did, that meant the world to me.

An appointment for me to audition was made and I turned up early and walked around the Southbank, silently going over my speech of *Richard III* and the 'gentleman caller' from Tennessee Williams' *The Glass Menagerie*. It seemed to go OK and I wasn't too nervous as I faced the line-up of nice, gentle people. A few weeks later they wrote to me, saying they had awarded me a scholarship! Not only that, but they also awarded me a living allowance over and above the grant. Oh how kind the Gods are when you struggle for something worthwhile!

And now for the second time in my life I had made my own steps and the cuffs were loosening. I became a man. I had trod the right path! I even had to open a bank account and I now had a cheque book, my first. Oh, eureka! In Picca-dilly Circus, of all places, since this is where the Arts Council deposited my money.

The day came, the first day. I took the tube from Manor House, kept on the Piccadilly Line to South Kensington and then walked up Brompton Road, SW7. A very pleasant tree-lined avenue and a turn right into a most beautiful old corner of London called Clareville Grove. At the end of the road was a large old house, The Webber Douglas School of Singing and Dramatic Art. I was a student, can you believe, a student, studying my art. How wonderful is that! And this craft would sustain me through thick and even thin for the rest of my life. I walked into the school on the first day and gathered up my scripts, the plays we would be studying and performing. I climbed some stairs and entered the room. I had arrived, I was there: never to look back, never to wonder, what shall I do? This is what I should do, this is what I should be: an actor.

The door closed and the lesson began.